Skirting the clearing, Cochrane and his people slowly closed the distance, and the team leader breathed a sigh of relief. But it was short-lived. Cochrane heard the voices first, just a few feet in front of him, then saw the enemy soldiers scrambling into their fighting positions as they brought up their weapons.

"Gooks! Get down!" he yelled, opening fire and spraying the enemy position to his immediate front. Orange clay kicked up around the bunkers just a few yards away. At that distance there was no time to aim. You just pointed and fired.

"Contact! Team 5-2, contact!" Andrus yelled into the radio's handset as he had been trained to, only to get no response. . . .

By Kregg P. J. Jorgenson

ACCEPTABLE LOSS: An Infantry Soldier's Perspective*
BEAUCOUP DINKY DAU
MIA RESCUE: LRRPs in Cambodia*

*Published by Ivy Books*

Books published by The Ballantine Publishing Group
are available at quantity discounts on bulk purchases
for premium, educational, fund-raising, and special
sales use. For details, please call 1-800-733-3000.

# MIA RESCUE

## LRRPs in Cambodia

### Kregg P. J. Jorgenson

### Foreword by Gary Linderer

IVY BOOKS • NEW YORK

Ivy Books
Published by Ballantine Books
Copyright © 1995 by Kregg P. J. Jorgenson
Excerpt from *Acceptable Loss* copyright © 1991 by
Kregg P. J. Jorgenson

http://www.randomhouse.com

Library of Congress Catalog Card Number: 95-95322

ISBN 0-8041-0980-X

Manufactured in the United States of America

First Ballantine Books Edition: June 1996

10  9  8  7  6  5  4  3  2  1

This book is dedicated to the memory of Rangers James F. McIntyre and Lyle Gayman, and to Apache Troopers Kit Beatton, Ron Aiman, and CSM Joseph Sparacino. Also to Doug Cochrane and my father, Keith H. Jorgenson, who died before this book appeared.

# CONTENTS

# FOREWORD

The Vietnam War was the greatest single divisive event in United States history since the American Civil War. During more than 10 years of U.S. involvement in South Vietnam, an entire generation of young Americans was forced to choose between supporting or not supporting the U.S. war effort. There was no middle ground, no buffer zone. The war affected each of us. The threat of the military draft hung over every male high school senior like an ominous specter. An event that in better times heralded a young man's passage into manhood became a sinister game of Russian roulette, a flip of the coin, a role of the dice. There was a general malaise in the air that kept us from feeling secure about our futures. Careers were put on back burners; many attended college who in ordinary times wouldn't have, while others dropped out under the pressure of maintaining grade points for all the wrong reasons; wedding plans were made prematurely and in other cases were canceled out of fear or uncertainty. Millions of young lives were kept in constant turmoil. Fear and doubt overshadowed enthusiasm and self-confidence. It was a traumatic time for America's youth, and an entire generation was at peril.

But this "baby boomer" generation did not abandon hope. In spite of the growing unpopularity of the Vietnam War and the soaring casualties that drained and wrecked the flower of this generation, its young men and women still answered our nation's call to duty. And they served with honor and courage in the face of an unpopular national cause that would have destroyed past generations.

Their personal sacrifices went unrecognized in the early years after the war. The few literary works that somehow found their way into the marketplace did so only because they were critical of the war . . . and of those who participated in it. A few Vietnam veterans speaking out against the war did manage to get their stories in print, but by and large the American public had had enough of Indochina. The war and its survivors were shoved to the back of the attic with the rest of life's unwanted baggage.

The time has now come to clean out the attic. A new generation of young Americans hungers for knowledge. They want to know why Vietnam is a "black hole" in our history. And they're intelligent enough to know that the truth and the lessons learned about the Vietnam War are not contained in the numerous volumes of buck-passing, finger-pointing literary trash marketed by the politicians, the diplomats, the journalists, and the military staff officers who were the real culprits in the Vietnam debacle. To the young men and women who paid their dues in blood and personal sacrifice on the deadly battlegrounds of Indochina, you are finally getting the chance to tell your stories. And for the first time, the pain and the trauma of a war not won are being revealed for those who will follow us.

Kregg Jorgenson is a survivor of the Vietnam War. A decorated warrior and an accredited journalist/author, he is uniquely qualified to write about combat in Vietnam. As in our court system, the credibility of an eyewitness is never challenged as circumstantial, nor is established expert testimony usually discredited. Kregg Jorgenson is both an eyewitness and an expert on the Vietnam War. His work needs no introduction, for it is honest, accurate, and well written, and what more can a reader ask for? He speaks for all of us survivors of Vietnam and especially those fallen comrades who can never tell their stories.

Gary Linderer
*Behind the Lines* magazine

# PREFACE

---

This book is based on the story of an ill-fated, five-man U.S. Army Ranger Long-Range Reconnaissance Patrol (LRRP, pronounced "lurp") missing in action in Cambodia in 1970 and the rescue mission that followed.

It is not the definitive history of the units involved, nor is it meant to be construed as the "official" version of what happened at the time. Instead, it is a war story told from the perspective of many of those who took part in the fighting.

The book itself was a two-year journey which allowed me to piece together the "real story" from a number of eye-witnesses and from documented accounts, which is why I say that it is not the official version.

Besides using the U.S. Army's records of the missions and various other documented accounts to give the tale additional credibility, I wanted to include the statements and comments of those who took part in the operation. So *MIA Rescue* is a story compiled from lengthy interviews, old notes, the recollections of participants, maps, and photos.

Unlike the U.S. Army's official after-action reports or lessons-learned formats, this story contains much human emotion. It is told from the point of view of several of the key players who were fighting on the ground or taking hostile fire in the air above, and not from those who later, calmly or indifferently, analyzed what had happened.

"The trouble with the official accounts is that they're

always too cut-and-dried, too black-and-white to really understand what had happened," explained a former helicopter pilot who took part in the rescue mission. "They don't have the feeling, color, or gut-level emotion that went into it. It's more than just boiled-down facts and figures; more than just that so many people were wounded or killed or how much equipment was lost or destroyed. That's for the number crunchers and the statisticians. When you tell the story," he said pointedly, "do us all a favor and make it breathe."

On a final note, *MIA Rescue* isn't about re-fighting the war in Vietnam in print and with vanity winning something that was lost years ago. It isn't about sanitizing history either, but humanizing it and making it breathe so the reader will get a better understanding of what occurred and what it took from those who were involved.

The honorable deeds of sometimes frightened but brave men deserve recognition, and after all of these years any praise is long overdue.

Kregg P. J. Jorgenson

# ACKNOWLEDGMENTS

There are a number of people I need to acknowledge for their encouragement and support with this project. Among them, I'd like to thank the members of the LRRP/Ranger Association of the 1st Cavalry Division (Vietnam War) and the members of Apache Troop, the 1st of the 9th Cav.

While much of this story came from after-action reports, newspaper accounts, POW/MIA records, and personal experience, it was the comments and interviews with the following people that provided important insight. Specifically, I'd like to cite Ron Andrus; Doug Cochrane; Lieutenant General Paul "Butch" Funk; Colonel George Paccerelli, U.S. Army, (Ret.); Colonel Clark Burnett, U.S. Army, (Ret.); Lieutenant Colonel Mike Brennan; Colonel Tom Fitzgerald, U.S. Army, (Ret.); John Bartlett; CSM Joe Sparacino; Norma Sparacino; Howard Shute; Eldon "Andy" Anderson; R. B. Alexander; Robert Edward Beal; Judy Beal; Kit Beatton; Jerome "Jerry" Boyle; Ron Black; Frank Duggan; John Williams; Art Dockter; Bill McIntosh; Louis Rochet; James F. McIntyre; Lyle Gayman; 1st Sergeant Frances Anthony Cortez; Rose Cortez; Jack Hugele; Glen Senkowski; Jim Braun; Cal Renfro; Ted Scherck; and Jon Varesko.

I'd also like to thank my editor at Ivy Books, Owen Lock, and his assistant, Ellen Key Harris, for their efforts. At Paladin Press, I'd like to gratefully acknowledge Jon

Ford and Paula Grano for their incredible efforts and enthusiasm.

Since I began this book, Joe Sparacino, James F. McIntyre, Lyle Gayman, Kit Beatton, Ron Aiman, Doug Cochrane and my father, Keith Henry Jorgenson, have died. Their guidance, friendship, and inspiration deserve more than these words. They are missed by those who knew and served with them.

Finally, I'd like to take the time to thank Richard Threlkeld of CBS for his field report that started it all. While there were a number of journalists in Vietnam during the war, there were probably only a few who, like Threlkeld, had the courage and empathy to go out on patrol with us to get a better understanding of the war.

Twenty-plus years later, the thank-yous are overdue.

# MIA RESCUE

# CHAPTER ONE

Hill #717
Mondol Kiri Province,
Cambodia, 17 June 1970
1650 hours

The sky was black and ominous, and the cloud cover threatened a heavy early-evening rain. Staff Sergeant Deverton Cochrane's assessment was just as dismal.

His five-man U.S. Army Ranger, long-range reconnaissance patrol, Team 5-2, had found the freshly dug bunkers and enemy fighting positions just inside the scrub-brush tree line atop the small rolling hill, and even though he had called a night halt, he regretted the decision, realizing this wasn't the place for the team to be for a few very good reasons.

First, night was closing and, second, so was the weather. That meant it was possible and damn likely for the North Vietnamese Army soldiers operating in the area to walk right up on the team without the team's noticing the enemy until it was too late. If the LRRP/Rangers had learned anything by then, it was that a new soldier from Hanoi was just as lost in the sprawling Cambodian and Vietnamese jungles as was a new soldier from Chicago. The NVA knew the locations of the bunker complexes in the region but little of the jungle that surrounded them. All of the myths about

1

NVA super jungle fighters to the contrary, in Southeast Asia, Daniel Boones on either side were few and far between.

"Saddle up," Cochrane whispered to the others, getting to his feet and shouldering a rucksack that held 70 or more pounds of explosive, antipersonnel mines, a spare battery for the team radio, trip flares, and damn near everything else that might come in handy in enemy territory. "We're moving out."

Just down the slope a few hundred meters away, a thick jungle patch offered more cover and concealment for their activities than the golf-course-like setting they found themselves in. Bright lime-green fields were edged with myriad green-and-brown interlocked plants and bushes. Hundred-foot trees watched over the dense woods like quiet onlookers, saying nothing of the traps and roughs.

He'd hide the team there, setting out claymore antipersonnel mines for their protection. Then he'd have Specialist Four Ron Andrus, the team's RTO (radio-telephone operator), put up the long whip antenna to keep in touch with the Ranger radio-relay station high atop Nui Ba Den, the Black Virgin Mountain in neighboring Vietnam, and the Ranger relay station at Fire Support Base David less than five miles away to the northeast.

If the team was compromised on patrol, their only chance for survival, besides their antipersonnel mines and individual weapons, was the backpack PRC-25 radio.

Andrus had called in their latest situation report a little over an hour before, and they weren't scheduled to call in again until 1720. The tearing static of the radio, the white noise of the empty frequency coming from the radio's handset close to his ear, was barely audible to him and couldn't be heard by the other members of the team who were studying the wall of jungle less than a few feet away.

While the rush of static might have been noise to some, it was satisfying to Andrus.

"We're moving down to the tree line," Cochrane whispered to Andrus and the others as he took the lead. The veteran staff sergeant kept the barrel of his M16 rifle aimed directly to his front as his eyes scanned the jungle clearing, searching in the twilight for sign of the enemy. Once satisfied, he began the slow, careful trek with Andrus in tow, followed by Specialist Four Carl Laker, the assistant team leader, Specialist Four Royce Clark, the team's medic, and finally, Staff Sergeant Dwight Hancock, the rear scout.

The job of a LRRP/Ranger was simple. Go behind the enemy lines in small five- or six-man teams, stick your nose in the enemy's business, and if you could, fuck with him.

Militarily, the job was defined in more strategic terms. The LRRP/Ranger's mission was, generally, to gather "hard" intelligence, that is, real proof of the enemy's strength, location, and movement. Best guesses weren't good enough; Army planners needed hard intelligence to plan for battles to come.

Fashioned after the British jungle-fighting teams of Malaysia and using the knowledge and tactics they themselves had learned from the Viet Cong, the LRRPs, as the Rangers were better known, began to enjoy the success of their commando-like patrols.

In jungles once thought of as safe havens by the soldiers of the North Vietnamese Army and the Viet Cong, the U.S. Army's LRRPs, in this instance the LRRP/Rangers of the 1st Cavalry Division, were ambushing their columns, snatching prisoners, or just monitoring their movement. The data thus gathered resulted in tremendous losses to the enemy forces, especially when the LRRPs themselves pinpointed the enemy's locations for artillery fire missions, the deadly gunnery of helicopter gunships and ground-attack aircraft, or bomb strikes.

When everything went well, the small teams did what they were asked to do and more. When everything went wrong, when it literally went to hell, it went to hell quickly because the five- and six-man teams were almost always outgunned, outnumbered, and well within territory controlled by the enemy.

If a team could repel a first attack using its claymore antipersonnel mines, devices that would literally send out a wall of ball bearings and heat blast from the explosion, then their rifles, grenades, and discipline would often be enough to keep the enemy at bay until the cavalry helicopter gunships or extraction helicopters arrived.

The one link that kept gunships or the artillery support from the nearby fire support base at their immediate call was the team's radio. But as Team 5-2 moved down the slope edging the shadowy tree line, Andrus had no way of knowing that the small valley they were walking into and the closing weather had made communication impossible. He and his team were in a dead zone, and until he could set up the long whip antenna, they could receive, but they couldn't be heard. This is because the transmitting stations he was listening for operated with a great deal more power than the PRC-25 he was using.

Skirting the clearing, Cochrane and his people slowly closed the distance, and the team leader breathed a sigh of relief. But it was short-lived. Cochrane heard the voices first, just a few feet in front of him, then saw the enemy soldiers scrambling into their fighting positions as they brought up their weapons.

"Gooks! Get down!" he yelled, opening fire and spraying the enemy position to his immediate front. Orange clay kicked up around the earth-and-tree-limb bunkers just a few yards away. At that distance, there was no time to aim. You just pointed and fired.

"Contact! Team 5-2, contact!" Andrus yelled into the radio's handset as he had been trained to, only to get no response. Firing a short burst of his rifle toward the enemy positions, Andrus quickly removed his rucksack and dug for the long whip antenna. His hands trembled but found what he was searching for anyway.

"Frag out!" Clark, the team medic, yelled, throwing a grenade into one of the nearby bunkers. The thundering explosion brought a momentary lull in the fighting. Taking full advantage of it, Andrus struggled with the olive-drab, folding metal pole, wiping away the mud from the wet ground.

Threading the longer antenna in place, Andrus was about to call again when the first Chinese grenade exploded to his left, sending hot, burning shrapnel fragments into his right shoulder. Fighting the pain, Andrus fired his rifle again, changed magazines, fired a second burst, and yelled into the radio one more time. "Bravo, Bravo . . . Team 5-2, contact!" he shouted, calling the relay station, his hand squeezing the radio handset so tight the pain hurt more than the shrapnel wound. There was no response from either relay station. Nothing. Team 5-2 was on its own.

The small battle continued with Cochrane up on one knee firing. "Back!" he yelled. "Move back!"

Raking machine-gun fire from the point-blank enemy positions swept across the Rangers' positions, and the team leader was the primary target. "I'm hit! Oh God! I'm . . ." he cried, as he dropped his weapon, then wordlessly slumped forward on his right shoulder. His head canted to the side as his hands struggled to hold in his life.

An arm's length away, Andrus started to reach for Cochrane just as a second explosion from another Chinese grenade shattered the attempt. Grenade fragments fractured his right wrist, and an armor-piercing bullet tore through the radio, burrowed easily into his collarbone and ripped deep into his chest, lodging dangerously close to his heart. What's happening? he thought. What in the hell's happening?

Laker, the assistant team leader, was yelling over the din of the firefight. "Did you get commo?" he screamed, only to have Andrus pull out of his momentary shock and say, "No," in a frustrated voice and bring his rifle back up again to fire. Instinct and training were taking over, overcoming both searing pain and fear.

"Fall back!" Laker said, motioning Andrus to move away from the kill zone, covering his retreat with M16 rifle fire. To their left, Clark saw an enemy soldier who had started to climb out of his fighting position. He stopped the man's advance permanently with a burst from his M14. Clark's quick response gave them a thin avenue out.

"Move!" Laker yelled seconds before the enemy machine-gun fire hit him and danced on to Clark, shattering his leg.

Staff Sergeant Dwight Hancock, the rear scout who had not moved into the kill zone because of his position in line, charged in, tossing a grenade into the bunker where the machine-gun fire was coming from, as Andrus and Clark returned fire while crawling out of the splintered ambush site.

"Bring the radio!" Hancock yelled, only to have Andrus say it wasn't any use; the armor-piercing round had left it a mess. He could see the broken parts through the hole in its casing. Crawling back, Andrus grabbed Laker's shoulder to pull him back as well, only to find that the left side of Laker's face from his forehead to his ear was blown away. Laker was dead, and the bloody fragments of what had once been the Ranger's face fell into Andrus' hand.

Turning back to Cochrane, the team's radioman could see

that the right side of the team leader's neck was ripped open, and blood covered the team leader's hands that held it firm but didn't move. The spurt of blood quickly reduced to a trickle.

Searching Laker's body for the URC-10, the team's emergency backup radio, Andrus changed magazines and opened fire as the tree line came alive. Judging by the sounds, the enemy was beginning his ground assault. Firing into the wall of moving foliage with one hand steadying his rifle, Andrus wildly sought out the backup radio with his other bloodied hand. But to no avail. Where is it? God, where is it?

Clark was writhing in pain but was somehow holding on. With his serious leg wound, he couldn't walk, let alone crawl, so Hancock lifted him on his back and carried him out of the kill zone while Andrus covered their retreat, scrambling after them in a slumping crouch and firing as he moved until his magazine was empty.

Forty meters down the darkened slope, Hancock had to put Clark down. He couldn't go any farther. Then, taking deep, labored breaths, he picked up the wounded medic a second time and tried once again to make good their E & E—escape and evasion.

Andrus was staggering behind them, turning back time and again in the now dark jungle evening, watching the enemy machine-gun fire and grenades tear orange and green shreds into the positions they had just left. He was trying to obliterate the LRRP's trail, but in the dark he couldn't tell how well he was doing. From the confusion back at the ambush site, it was clear that the NVA didn't know where the Americans were. But if Andrus returned fire, he would give the team's position away. So following Hancock's lead, Specialist Four Ron Andrus swore to himself and then reluctantly turned away after the rear scout. There was nothing he could do for either Cochrane or Laker and as he withdrew, his wounds were more than the shrapnel and bullet lodged in his body.

Sixty yards or so farther, they knew they couldn't go on. Clark was in too much pain, and Andrus' chest was growing tight from the bullet wound. His lungs burned but not as much as the trail the bullet had left in its wake. Finding cover in waist-high brush, they took a quick assessment.

They had taken four casualties: two left in the kill zone and most likely dead, and two who couldn't move much farther. With only two rifles, 15 magazines, no grenades, and no radios, what was left of Team 5-2 was wondering what to do next. Of course, the North Vietnamese Army soldiers knew exactly what they'd do: after discovering their success and licking their own wounds, they'd quickly police the kill zone, collect the bodies of the Rangers and their equipment, then hurriedly move out of the immediate area to wait for the arrival of the gunships that almost always followed a contact with the soldiers with painted faces. Twenty minutes or so later, when no artillery thundered in on their positions and when no helicopters arrived to harass them, the NVA would begin to realize their good fortune: nobody was coming for the Rangers.

Even though the sun had set and the rain was beginning to fall hard against the jungle, the enemy would begin his search. The odds were in his favor. The Rangers had gambled one too many times, and the soldiers of the North Vietnamese Army would show them just how much they had lost. If not this evening, then certainly in the morning.

# CHAPTER TWO

Even before the sun came up on May 1, 1970, scout helicopters and gunships from the United States Army's 1st Cavalry Division were leading the invasion into Cambodia. Their targets were the Viet Cong's headquarters command and the vast weapons storehouses, equipment centers, and North Vietnamese Army bases just inside the border regions of the neighboring "neutral" country.

Striking out of Tay Ninh, Binh Long, and Phuoc Long provinces of South Vietnam, the Cav was joined by combined American forces and the South Vietnamese Army as they pushed quickly and menacingly into the enemy strongholds.

Three key areas were singled out and became the focus of the attack, and the battles for these regions took on the names of their map characteristics: the Fishhook, the Parrot's Beak, and the Angel's Wing. There, entire enemy divisions trained and operated openly, flaunting their indifference to the Sihanouk regime of Cambodia. Not that Cambodian sovereignty mattered much to the strategists behind the invasion; Sihanouk was a fence-straddler who often played one enemy against another as it suited his purpose.

The American objective was simple: strike a crippling blow against Ho Chi Minh's army and force Hanoi into a negotiated peace.

The "invasion," in reality a raid, for the most part caught the communist forces off guard and sent the Viet Cong and North Vietnamese Army units retreating for safety and cover. While the enemy command suspected the Americans were up to something, they didn't believe it would be a sustained drive, let alone react in time to save more than face.

In the first three days of the operation, the NVA and Viet Cong not only lost their once-safe havens and sanctuaries for the main infiltration routes into South Vietnam, but they also lost much of their military muscle in the form of crucial supplies, equipment, arms, ammunition, and manpower in the region. Most military historians agree that the raid set back the enemy's strategic goals and battle objectives by 18 to 36 months.

In one well-hidden Viet Cong jungle base alone, over 11,000 underground living quarters and warehouses were discovered and captured. Nicknamed The City because of its immense size and proportions, this maze of interlocked fighting positions, training sites, storehouses, and compounds demonstrated the degree to which the Viet Cong battalions and North Vietnamese Army counterparts relied on the area for the preparation and supply of military operations in South Vietnam.

Publicly, Hanoi adamantly stated time and again that it had neither soldiers nor bases in Cambodia, when in fact the North Vietnamese were squeezing more than just their admitted South Vietnamese enemies. To keep the Cambodian monarch in line, they trained and armed the Khmer Rouge and held them on a short leash. All the while, tons of Vietnamese communist war equipment and thousands of soldiers a day flowed from the north into Cambodia for eventual infiltration south down a series of well-marked jungle highways and routes that was world famous as the Ho Chi Minh Trail.

In addition to the land routes, the Viet Cong and NVA

used Cambodian rivers and seaports to ship in more war materials. The steady stream of men and munitions was vital to the North's goal, and although B-52 bomb strikes had hindered the enemy's procession, they weren't enough to bring it to a halt.

It was no secret that many of the preinvasion rocket and mortar attacks and the elaborately staged ground assaults against American outposts and base camps originated in Cambodia, or that the infiltration routes led directly back across the border. Gunship pilots and scout reconnaissance helicopters reported seeing the enemy flee into Cambodia almost daily.

Using the boundary lines of neutral Cambodia as a shield, the NVA and Viet Cong commands planned, trained for, supplied, and conducted their operations virtually unchecked. Using hit-and-run tactics, the communists struck at the Americans and their allies before retreating across the border, where they would regroup, replan, and strike again.

On the surface, the border sanctuaries and hidden bases appeared to be a matter of mutual political convenience for North Vietnam and Cambodia, which had aligned itself with China for its own agenda and purpose. Turning a blind eye to traditional intrusions and animosities became necessary for survival and strategic positioning.

But the two neighboring nations were playing a deadly manipulative game of historic chess. In private deals and arrangements with the West, Prince Norodom Sihanouk secretly authorized the clandestine American bombing missions against the Viet Cong and North Vietnamese Army bases in his country. Known as Operation MENU, the covert bombing missions were Sihanouk's private revenge on the Vietnamese interlopers and their less than subtle or veiled threats. Sihanouk's trump card lay in his friendship with the Chinese who were also traditional enemies of the Vietnamese. Because of their more than *2,000 years* of enmity, any alliance between North Vietnam and China was shaky at best, a fact which was well understood in both Beijing and Hanoi.

As early as the end of World War II, Ho Chi Minh understood that it was better to bring the colonialist French back into his country than allow expansion or encroachment by the Chinese. The communist leader summed up the collective feeling this way: "It is better," he said, "to eat dung from the French for a hundred years than it is from the Chinese for another thousand years!" Old hostilities die hard, and Vietnam was still very nationalistic despite its socialist ties to its more powerful neighbor to its north.

Sihanouk knew this, and by playing his traditional enemies against each other, he hoped to pressure the Vietnamese into leaving their sanctuaries within Cambodia's borders without having to confront them openly. His was a balancing act that sooner or later had to fail, but while it was in play, he allowed the Viet Cong and North Vietnamese to use the region as a training and transit point. The ploy would prove costly for the prince and the Cambodian people.

Norodom Sihanouk was overthrown by Prime Minister Lon Nol early in 1970. The coup had been backed by the West, and Lon Nol gave President Richard Nixon of the United States authorization to conduct more than just clandestine bombing missions. Nol agreed to the raid or limited invasion led, in theory, by the South Vietnamese Army but backed by the more powerful American forces.

An avowed anticommunist and old enemy of the Vietnamese, North and South, Nol saw the raid as a viable way of knocking out the communist sanctuaries within his nation's borders and of dealing a blow to the North Vietnamese and Viet Cong, who were reluctant to leave.

In fact, most Cambodians harbored hard feelings for the Vietnamese who, in their view, had literally stolen what became South Vietnam from the ancient Khmer empire. The Vietnamese, of course, saw themselves as simply having won the territory, but the Cambodians still felt they had simply stolen it. Now the Cambodians saw the North Vietnamese bases along the Ho Chi Minh Trail as simply another attempt to carve more territory from Cambodia.

Lon Nol saw the attack against the Vietnamese interlopers as a way to right some very old wrongs. Since Sihanouk had been placed in power as the ruling monarch by the French, it was also a subtle way to show the colonialists, even the Americans, that Cambodia was for Cambodians, and that they alone would determine their destiny.

But adventurous ploys require unlikely partnerships, so the ancient struggles would continue only with a few new players and for considerably higher stakes.

Militarily, the 61-day raid would be a success for the South Vietnamese and the Americans, although the venture would become unimaginably complex for all of the figures involved. Sihanouk would flee to exile in China, while the Viet Cong and NVA would temporarily lose their infiltration bases and springboard into South Vietnam. The operation would also create increased problems for Richard Nixon in the United States and, ultimately, prove disastrous for the Cambodian people, who would suffer the blood-stained genocidal purge of the communist Khmer Rouge.

For those who took part in the raid, it would prove to be an empty victory for a cause that wasn't worth the effort. While it would severely hinder the military capabilities of the North Vietnamese Army in the South, the North's staggering losses would only be temporary. Men and equipment could be replaced. But the North Vietnamese understood that sooner or later the Americans would give up and go home, just as the French had done before them, the Japanese before them, and the Chinese before them.

Then the Vietnamese would win, even if they suffered great losses in the process.

Back in the United States, the American people had long lost heart in the prolonged war, and the Cambodian incursion would only escalate their impatience with it.

Over 300 Americans would die in the raid, and another 1,500 would sustain serious injuries. And always at the head of the fighting and bearing the brunt of those numbers were the 1st Cavalry Division's reconnaissance units—most notably units such as H Company Rangers, the Cav's behind-the-lines, long-range patrols, and the helicopter attack troops of the 1st of the 9th.

# CHAPTER THREE

They were young, cocky, and very good at what they did, which was pull dangerous, long-range patrols behind enemy lines. They were the Cav's LRRPs and the Army's answer to Marine Force Recon and Navy SEAL teams in the jungles of South Vietnam. For the most part they were 19- and 20-year-old soldiers, volunteers doing a job that few wanted or relished because of the tasks they had to perform.

Because of the dangers of the job and, mostly, because of their successes, allowances were made for, well, a certain amount of unorthodox behavior when in the rear. In fact, in an Army division otherwise bent on uniformity, they were permitted to carry exotic weapons and captured weapons. They sported black berets and camouflage fatigues with a unique red-white-and-black scroll-like patch above their division patch that made them stand out among the other soldiers. But then maybe what made them distinct was more than their weapons and uniforms.

Their critics, and they had many, called them "hot dogs" and "prima fucking donnas," but even the critics—like the Viet Cong and NVA soldiers the LRRPs hunted— begrudgingly admitted the LRRPs were good.

Call signs were changed frequently, but in 1969 they became SLASHING TALON and kept the radio name. Initially, the change of the call signs was used to confuse the

Viet Cong and North Vietnamese Army, who monitored the American radio transmissions, while keeping the SLASHING TALON name became a new way and a weapon used to instill fear in the enemy units operating in the Cav's area of operations. They operated in small five-man teams, and in five years of combat service in Southeast Asia, the men of Hotel Company, 75th Infantry, became the highest-decorated unit of its kind in American history.

Although they could trace their lineage back to the Ranger or reconnaissance companies of earlier wars, supporting their claim with a loose-link, bastard connection to Rogers' Rangers of pre-Revolutionary America, the story of the Cav's LRRPs actually began in the late '60s. The unit first appeared as LRRP Detachment, 191st Military Intelligence (MI), and it was used to counter the harassing tactics of the Viet Cong militia. Stymied by the shockingly effective guerrillas of the well-organized National Liberation Front, American military strategists discovered that by using commando tactics of their own—tactics fashioned after British Commando operations in Malaysia—the U.S. Army's own Special Forces successes in country, and even the stratagems of the enemy, they could turn the tables on the seemingly elusive Viet Cong and, later, the hard-core North Vietnamese Army soldiers.

From north to south, South Vietnam was divided into four corps tactical zones (CTZs; or MRs, military regions), numbered I, from south of the demilitarized zone (DMZ), through IV, in the Mekong Delta. Operating out of Camp Evans in the I Corps section of South Vietnam, the small long-range recon patrols could screw with the enemy in much the same way the enemy operated.

The Cav's LRRPs could track their enemy to determine his numbers, types, strengths, and weaknesses; snatch (capture alive) enemy prisoners who traveled the jungle trails; spring ambushes in the enemy's own backyard; and call in air and artillery strikes. In short, the Cav's LRRPs were an invaluable source of much needed military intelligence about enemy troop concentrations and activities. And using their radios, they could call down the wrath of God—in the form of supporting aviation and artillery—on enemy forces.

With a handful of such LRRP companies attached to combat divisions and forward combat elements, the Army could now get a better handle on understanding the enemy it faced. From high mountain terrain up north in I Corps to the swampy Delta in IV Corps, the LRRPs were carving out very fearsome reputations one deadly mission at a time.

While saving the Vietnamese from communism must have seemed like a reasonable, even admirable, goal to the policymakers in Washington, D.C., the facts on the ground revealed that the goal wasn't possible. The enemy the LRRPs faced was more determined than his South Vietnamese counterparts. Hard history lessons were being learned daily, and the tests were measured in the numbers of soldiers wounded or killed. In a battle, the success of which had to be measured in "hearts and minds" won rather than by territory gained, Vietnam was proving to be a country of hardened hearts and stubborn minds that were anything but collective.

The small Southeast Asian country wasn't one culture but a myriad of them with pronounced ethnic diversities and centuries of established hatreds and animosities. Besides the Vietnamese there were the Chams, the Cambodian Khmers, Nung Chinese, and those the French had mislabeled as Montagnards, the tribal "mountain people," whom the Vietnamese of both sides considered *moi*, savages.

Then, too, there were disaffected South Vietnamese nationalists who were not communists. This made matters more complex because even though many people had the same goals or political beliefs, many nationalists and even some communists in the South distrusted the communists in the North. There were also a number of religious groups in the country, such as the Cao Dai who were distrusted by the government in the South and hated the VC, who were responsible for the death of the sect's founder.

The Buddhists were suspicious of the ruling Catholics who were just as suspicious of the Cao Dai. Enmity ran so strong that the Cao Dai of Tay Ninh maintained private armies, large well-armed and well-trained armies, to protect themselves and their right to practice their own religion.

So powerful were the Cao Dai that leaders from Saigon and Hanoi both vied for their support. During this new Vietnam War, it was difficult for Americans to tell the players apart without a scorecard. Unfortunately, the scorecards hadn't been written yet, and because of the local rules, it wasn't uncommon for the players to changes sides in the middle of the game.

The Americans and their allies were just beginning to understand the complexity of the problems they faced in Vietnam and were scrambling to readjust their thinking as well as their tactics.

Although the politics of the war were giving the policymakers headaches, some relief came in the form of small successes and lessons *truly* learned, that is, they led to new tactics, such as the establishment of LRRP companies, the adoption of proper small-unit tactics, and aerial rifle platoons.

The Cav's LRP detachment was formed in November 1966 when MG. John Norto selected a twenty-eight-year-old Special Forces captain named Jame D. James to form the unit at division headquarters in An Khe. By February 1967 the LRP detachment became LRRP, with an extra R. The Long-Range Patrol Unit now became the Long-Range Reconnaissance Patrol Unit. While the change seemed like a minor difference to probably everybody except the Vietnamese tailor who sewed on the new patches, the name change reflected the company's new role as a reconnaissance unit, that is, intelligence collector.

On December 20, 1967, the unit underwent yet another name change, becoming Company E (LRP), 52d Infantry. The name changes reflected the way the U.S. Army conducted its war, adjusting to new strategies and reacting to the adjustments. The Cav's LRRPs had gained a certain amount of status and recognition for their jungle patrols, the effects of which were being felt by the Viet Cong and North Vietnamese Army units who now no longer felt secure in their own jungle bases or once-safe rear areas.

Used to counteract enemy activity in the region by providing the division with much needed hard intelligence, Company E proved surprisingly successful in jungle-fighting operations, beating the enemy at his own jungle war.

Because E Company fell under the umbrella of the division's foremost combat squadron, the 1st of the 9th, there was a move by some to incorporate the company into the squadron officially and redesignate it as E Troop.

In 1968, a former Special Forces Team Leader, Captain George Paccerelli of Colville, Washington, was brought in to do just that. A mustang officer, that is, one who worked his way up through the enlisted ranks, Paccerelli arrived with Infantry, Airborne, and Special Forces combat experience.

He had earned his first Combat Infantryman's Badge with the Green Berets in Laos during Operation WHITE STAR in 1962. After going on to Officer's Candidate School and earning his commission, Paccerelli went back to combat, this time as a Special Forces A-Team leader at Dak Sam in 1966. In this assignment, Paccerelli had been bayoneted while leading a charge on a fortified enemy position. In the hectic jungle battle, the lieutenant killed the enemy soldier and turned back toward the objective, only to be shot in the arm moments later.

By the time he arrived at Company E (LRRP), the newly promoted captain was a seasoned veteran with years of experience—experience that would give him the edge over the other officers who applied for the job.

"I wanted the company so badly that I would have told the squadron commander anything to get the job!" explained Paccerelli. "I knew that the company had potential and that by tapping into it, we'd have one hell of a unit." Which is exactly what Paccerelli did. Taking what he had learned as part of the elite and misnamed Vietnam Studies and Observation Group, the Special Forces SOG, Paccerelli set up a difficult and demanding three-week, in-country jungle training course. He then went about recruiting the most qualified and enthusiastic soldiers from the division's replacement center or from other units.

More stringent rules and regulations began to find their way into the new changeover and little by little the division began to reap the benefits of the transition.

"We had some unbelievable talent in the company, I mean, E-4 and E-5 team leaders who surpassed most line officers' combat qualifications or skills," said Paccerelli.

As a result, E Company took on the additional responsibility of training other reconnaissance units within the division in patrolling, that is, small unit operations. Lessons truly learned could not go unheeded.

When the Cav moved south to III Corps and into the heart of War Zone C to disrupt the flow of enemy infiltration and activity, the 80-man company made its home at Camp Gorvad in Phuoc Vinh. Working out of the forward base camp, they monitored and harassed the 1st and the 7th North Vietnamese Army elements and the 5th and 9th Viet Cong battalions that made the region their home.

By February 1969, after 15 months of what the Army

called "outstanding" success, and in a move to regulate and coordinate LRRP operations, MACV (Military Assistance Command Vietnam) reactivated the 75th Infantry (Ranger) as the umbrella organization that contained all the legitimate LRRP companies.

For the 75th Infantry, 13 companies were formed from the LRRP units in country, and although they shared a common purpose, they remained independent of each other, subordinate still to the divisions or combat units with which they worked. A command in name only, the 75th Infantry LRRP/Rangers were still on their own. General Creighton W. Abrams, the MACV commander, gave the official nod to the Ranger plan, and in doing so, he once again established the tradition of nontradition long associated with the 75th Infantry Rangers. Activated in each preceding war only to be deactivated shortly after the fighting was over, the 75th Infantry Rangers seemed to have but one real purpose: combat. The Vietnam War would be no exception.

Tolerated but not officially authorized were the large red-white-and-black shoulder scrolls that read AIRBORNE RANGER. The black berets, Merrill's Marauders pocket flash, the job description provided the common thread for the 13 new Ranger companies.

SOPs, the standard operating procedures for the companies, hadn't been set in stone, and the division or field force units that had their own LRRPs utilized them as they saw fit. Some companies operated 30-man (platoon-size) patrols, while the others opted for anything from four- to 10-man patrols. The 1st Cav's LRRPs, known as H Company, used the five-man team, reasoning that the smaller team had a smaller chance of being detected by the enemy. Of course, that also meant a smaller proportion of a team could react to the enemy if the team took some wounded during a mission. For example, if one man were badly wounded, he'd need at least one man to help him E & E; that would leave only three weapons to return fire on the enemy. But it was felt that with any small patrol, trade-offs were a necessity and that, for Hotel Company's purposes, five men was about optimum.

The reason for the company's success wasn't a unique approach to reconnaissance operations as much as it was a well-planned and carefully considered decision. But then, Hotel Company approached many, even the most minor, of its concerns with similar care. For instance, on Hotel Company's 75th Ranger scroll, the words read RANGER AIRBORNE instead of AIRBORNE RANGER because Lieutenant Michael Brennan, a platoon leader with the company, argued that "not everyone in the company ... was Airborne or parachute qualified. However, after their in-country and subsequent evaluation, they would be LRRP qualified." That is, they became Rangers before they qualified as Airborne. The deciding minds agreed with Brennan's assessment, and Hotel Company carved out its own niche in the history of the 75th Rangers by slightly altering its shoulder patch.

Indeed, not everyone in the company was Airborne qualified, let alone Fort Benning Ranger trained. Volunteers were usually recruited from the division's replacement station or from the infantry reconnaissance units the LRRPs had helped train. After recruitment, the would-be LRRPs were put through a rigorous two-week training program that, in reality, lasted three weeks.

Housed in a platoon-size tent, the new LRRP trainees were kept apart from the company's personnel and underwent a difficult and busy training course with hours of classroom work that gave way to hands-on training and practical application. It wasn't uncommon for infantry soldiers on watch at the base camp's perimeter guard bunkers to be left speechless as they watched the LRRP recruits go through their predawn runs along the perimeter road each morning or dangle on 75-foot ropes beneath helicopters, practicing their quick jungle-exit McGuire rig extractions. The LRRP trainees who made the cut would use this type of extraction time and again to bewilder and confuse their Vietnamese enemies.

Thrown in for good measure were demanding conditioning drills and a heavy dose of harassment. The unit had to be certain that the new volunteers could cut it as LRRPs under the extraordinarily tense conditions of real LRRP missions, and the only way to ensure that was to put them through the mill to grind them into acceptable replacements.

The training was intense and, at times, very difficult, and more than half of the trainees in each training cycle failed the program, while others, including Stateside Fort Benning, Georgia, trained Rangers would quit in frustration.

The standards were high, but the company's leadership argued that they had to be. "With a five-man team in jungle combat, you couldn't afford mistakes. You had to be sure you could rely on the other members in the team. Failing or passing a required test was not just a question of academics," said Robert Edward Beal, a former member of Hotel Company from Greensboro, North Carolina. "It often meant the difference between living and dying."

Of course, war being war, even successfully completing the training regimen did not ensure longevity on the battlefield because of the hazardous nature of the job. In five years of combat duty, more than 30 team members would be killed in action, and nearly 40 percent of the company would be wounded in action.

"The training had to be realistic and pertinent to the theater of operations, and I believe that it was the quality of the training that led to the company's success," added Beal.

The LRRP recruits were schooled in small-unit tactics, map reading, artillery coordination, ambush techniques, rappelling, Viet Cong and North Vietnamese Army procedures and operations, and a variety of other related subject material that directly applied to Southeast Asia. They were also cross-trained as radio-telephone operators and team medics.

Periodically, the training was carried on in the field, and it was sometimes punctuated with enemy rocket or mortar attacks, sniper fire, perimeter defense against ground probes or all-out assaults, or other real-world situations when the war refused to yield to the LRRP program.

Officially, the course was two weeks in length with 216 hours of formal training; in fact, it continued well into the third week. According to one training NCO, "There was always something more to teach the trainees, something we'd learn from our patrols and incorporate into the training."

Upon graduation and a brief ceremony, the new LRRPs were assigned to the company teams and to one of the two platoon-size barracks that housed them. Sometimes the new graduates would have only minutes to store their personal effects before being told they'd be going out the next day on a team and to report to their team leader for an OP (operation) order.

It was rare that a new LRRP had to wait the required 90 days to earn the Combat Infantryman's Badge or even a Purple Heart; sometimes a new LRRP earned both on his first outing, only days after joining a team.

Consider Jim McIntyre's first patrol. After a five-day mission in the jungles around Quan Loi, the quiet Chittenango, New York, resident was relieved to have completed the patrol when he jumped aboard an extraction helicopter. Sitting in the open bay door as the helicopter dipped its nose and lifted off the landing zone, McIntyre's relief gave way to anxiety when the helicopter shuddered violently and seconds later emitted a terrible mechanical scream.

"We cleared the landing zone and were just above the trees when something went wrong. The next thing I know, we were tumbling towards the ground."

When he finally came to, McIntyre tried to get to his feet but wasn't having much luck. His head was pounding, and he didn't have to fight to remain conscious.

The downed helicopter, or what was left of it, lay tangled and twisted in the splintered crash site. The pilot had managed to send out a call for help as the aircraft was falling, and a rescue force was hurriedly dispatched to assist. McIntyre and two other survivors were medevacked out and flown to a nearby fire support base for immediate medical treatment. But care would be slow in coming because that same evening, the small jungle base was hammered by a barrage of mortar rounds, which was followed by a North Vietnamese Army unit's human-wave ground attack, its infantrymen charging the barbed-wire perimeter, desperately trying to overrun the remote outpost.

By dawn the enemy withdrew, leaving many of his wounded and dead behind. The attack had failed, and the base was licking its wounds. As was the new LRRP. When McIntyre finally made it back to the company headquarters in Phuoc Vinh two days later, even the Ranger company commander, Captain George Paccerelli, felt the young Ranger's first mission might have been too tough. Captain Paccerelli offered McIntyre a transfer to a safer job outside the company, but the determined young Ranger refused.

His decision would prove to be to the company's advantage; while on another patrol, McIntyre earned a Silver Star for gallantry in action during a firefight when he managed to throw his rucksack on a live grenade, angling the heavy pack to deflect the explosion while yelling for the rest of the team to take cover.

Even the division commander had to admit it was one of the bravest and most intelligent acts he had heard of a soldier doing, since the rucksack absorbed much of the grenade's explosion and shrapnel.

McIntyre downplayed the action, and although he would be among the first to point to others in the unit who deserved more recognition or merit, his actions typified the kind and caliber of those who served in Hotel Company.

To some outsiders, the company seemed to be a glory-seeking unit, but those who really understood Hotel Company's mission and area of operations realized the unit was an indispensable part of the 1st Cav's strategy and of its intelligence apparatus. And that the "glory" came at considerable risk and cost. If the training was difficult, it was because the patrols and missions were even more so. Besides being difficult, the missions were extremely dangerous and, for the most part, just plain uncomfortable.

On the five-day long-range patrols there were no hot meals, no change of clothes, or even time to relax. Uniforms remained buttoned to the neck, sleeves buttoned at the wrists, and camouflage paint covered the exposed areas of the hands, neck, and face.

Besides the web gear that held their ammunition and grenades, the LRRPs carried 60- to 100-pound rucksacks that pulled at their shoulders and backs as they slowly, carefully worked their way through the dense jungles and rain forests. In the tropical, sometimes staggering heat, even uniforms and rucksacks became opponents to contend with.

In the evening, they'd set up a night-halt position, sitting up and forming a circle as the dark closed in around them. They slept in shifts, pulling guard duty in one-hour increments and rotating the job to the next team member in line.

Nobody spoke unnecessarily, and required communication was done in hushed whispers or with hand signals. Because of the noise they made, no air mattresses, rain ponchos, or shelter halves kept the LRRPs safe from the elements. When it rained, which was frequent, the LRRPs took being wet in reluctant stride.

At sunset, when the heat from the Vietnamese day could no longer work its way through the layer after living layer of intertwined vegetation and the monsoon rains fell, the rain-soaked LRRPs derived some (very) small degree of satisfaction from the knowledge that at least the rain discouraged the swarms of mosquitoes that otherwise would surround and attack them; during drier periods, the mosquito swarms were so thick that it wasn't uncommon for LRRPs to inhale the creatures as they breathed.

On patrol, the LRRP teams walked in a prescribed formation with the point (first) man carefully watching 180 degrees to his front, while the second man watched and covered the right side of the jungle. The third LRRP protected the left flank, and the fourth man faced the opposite direction, leaving the last team member or rear scout to cover their movement from the rear. Careful to avoid detection, they avoided trails and worked to cover their own direction of movement. After all, the odds were never in the LRRP's favor, and there was no need to give NVA or Viet Cong patrols any more advantage.

Over the course of the mission, they'd patrol a 4,000- to 5,000-meter area searching for signs of the enemy and gathering information as they went. When they came upon a recently used trail or bunker complex, the small patrol would monitor the area while setting up claymore antipersonnel mines in a defensive perimeter to form a wall of exploding protection if needed.

If a small enemy force happened to walk down a trail that the patrol was monitoring, the Rangers sprang their ambush, initiating it with the deadly crescent-shaped claymore antipersonnel mines and following it up with aimed fire into the kill zone. The LRRPs would capture any wounded enemies who had been lucky enough to survive and then collect any equipment, papers, weapons, and other items that might offer intelligence data to the division. Documents were particularly valuable, as they might identify units in the area, coming actions, rosters of Communist Party cadre masquerading as ordinary civilians, and so forth.

If a force much larger than the LRRPs was encountered, the small Ranger team would monitor its direction of movement, noting any pertinent characteristics about the unit that the intelligence people would need to determine a strategy and course of action.

On one such encounter, a team found a well-used jungle trail that was hidden from the air by the dense foliage and triple-layer canopy of the tropical rain forest. These "trails," which were sometimes a series of well-constructed and well-maintained roads, also hid the movement of enemy soldiers and supplies to the region. Although the hard-packed orange route this team found was the width of a city sidewalk, it displayed signs of recent enemy use. Boot prints were fresh. Their edges were still sharp and distinct, as were the deep bicycle tire tracks that told the Rangers that the enemy was using bicycles to transport munitions or equipment.

Quickly and quietly, several of the team members set up a series of claymore mines in a protective perimeter that, if needed, would send out thousands of small bearings in a steel wall against the enemy. The three remaining team members guarded their movements. Then, the team waited as the shrieks, grunts, and cries of the jungle life around them—the many birds, monkeys, and animals that inhabited the rain forest—settled into an awkwardly dark evening. As the last rays of sunlight gave way to the damp black curtain of night, the first sounds of enemy movement filtered through the underbrush. Metal was hitting against metal—maybe canteens or slings on their weapons. Nothing

loud, but distinct enough to let the Ranger team know the
enemy was close and heading in the team's direction.

It wasn't long after dark when the Ranger team's rear
scout noticed in the distance the first pale yellow glow of
a flashlight heading their way. Squeezing the arm of the
next LRRP in line, the rear scout whispered his find, and
his team member immediately relayed the news to the team
leader next to him.

The North Vietnamese Army point man was leading the
NVA down the winding jungle route directly in front of the
American Rangers, unaware that four M16s and one AK-47
were aimed at his chest. The Rangers held their fire, while
ribbons of yellow lights bobbed and bounced from the line
of soldiers that followed the point man.

"The trail was less than four yards away, and we counted
10 NVA soldiers, at first," said Sergeant Johnny Rodriguez,
the LRRP team leader with Hotel Company in 1970.
"Then, the rest of them came. NCOs and officers were
moving up and down the steady line of soldiers, yelling at
them in the process."

The tense moment peaked as an enemy soldier walking
between the claymore antipersonnel mines and the Ranger
team caught his boot on the plastic-covered wire that led
from the series of mines to the team leader, whose heart
was pounding. Cursing, the Vietnamese soldier kicked the
wire away and continued moving, perhaps thinking it was
little more than a vine.

Rodriguez, counting every passing shadow, estimated the
enemy force at over 300. Long after they had passed and
the jungle grew quiet again, the team remained on alert and
on edge over what had just occurred. A usually gregarious
soldier, Rodriguez remained tense and stone-faced while he
retold the event at the team's debriefing.

Since the odds were against them, contact was to be
avoided. Reconnaissance patrols were just that, and it was

much easier to plan strategy against an enemy when the enemy didn't know he was being watched. When contact did occur and the teams found it necessary to fight, they reacted with fast and furious small-arms fire.

In these sudden encounters, when the teams came face-to-face with enemy soldiers on jungle trails, they went into well-rehearsed escape and evasion drills. The first LRRP to make contact would fire a full 20-round magazine from his M16 in the directions of contact and make a hasty retreat while the remaining team members followed suit, repeating the process until contact was broken or until they safely made their escape.

While training and professionalism lowered the odds against them, contact was still a matter of chance and very much a risk. The difference, some said, came from the determination of the Rangers themselves. Contrary to the public's perception, few who served with Hotel Company could be described as old, grizzled veterans, or even the John Wayne or John Rambo types. Many were 19- and 20-year-olds who looked as though they belonged somewhere else. Ron Saunders of Marysville, Washington, was so clean-cut and young-looking that the Vietnamese dubbed him "Baby-san." Then, too, there were young Rangers like Howard Shute of Munhall, Pennsylvania, Dick Cramer of Redondo Beach, California, and Jon Varesko of Rices Landing, Pennsylvania, who looked as though they would have been more at home in a high school homeroom than involved in an Army Ranger unit in combat. But appearances are deceptive. While John Wayne rode across the silver screen bigger than life, real-life characters, such as Saunders, Cramer, Shute, Varesko, and many other young soldiers in the company, were acting out real-life dramas, living or dying in scenarios that Hollywood had yet to imagine.

Cal Renfro of Seattle, Washington, was a team leader who ambushed a six-man NVA patrol only to discover that it was a point element of a much larger communist force. In the fierce and hectic battle that followed, Renfro and his team set several quick, running ambushes on the North Vietnamese Army soldiers who pursued his team.

The frustrated and determined NVA soldiers chased the team well into the night, and Renfro, knowing the team was almost out of ammunition, called for an extraction helicopter. Calling a halt, Renfro set up a makeshift perimeter and radioed in their position. When the helicopter arrived on station, he held up a strobe light for the helicopter crew to fix their exact location. As the team was setting up for a McGuire rig extraction, in which the rescue helicopter lowers ropes down through the jungle and then yanks the Rangers almost literally out of the enemy's hands, an enemy point man opened up on the team leader. The automatic-rifle burst shot the small strobe light out of Renfro's hand but missed the Ranger, who then killed the point man. The battle resumed. Then Renfro and the team were pulled through the trees from the frightening night firefight, while the enemy fired blindly into the dark sky and surrounding rain forest.

If the Ranger teams and their patrols became the subject of many war stories, then so did the actions of those who led them. Of the 12 company commanders who led the unit over the course of the war, perhaps none was more respected or admired than Paccerelli, but not always for his combat experience. For instance, there was the time when two of the company's team leaders were arrested in Phuoc Vinh after an altercation with the Military Police and a wild chase through the dust-blown back alleys and dirt streets of the former French plantation village. "We were in between missions on stand down and we had a pass to go into the village, so another team leader and I opted to spend some time in an off-limits establishment," explained Renfro, grinning. "A bar/whorehouse. Anyway, the MPs raided it, and we found ourselves scrambling to get away. We went over fences, down alleys, and in and out of buildings before the MPs managed to cut us off."

Arrested and handcuffed, the two LRRPs were thrown in the back of a jeep and driven back to the company compound, where they were brought before Paccerelli.

"When he came out of the orderly room, he took a look at us and another at the arrest report and then yelled at the MP in charge to immediately release us. When that was done, he ripped up the report in front of the MPs and literally chased them from the compound area.

"He told them that was no way to treat his Rangers, and we were grinning, locking our heels at attention." Renfro added that while the stunned MPs watched, the commander chewed out the team leaders, not only for being in an off-limits establishment, but also for getting caught by the MPs. " 'You're LRRPs! You're not supposed to get caught!' Paccerelli yelled. It's a lesson that neither the other team leader nor I ever forgot," Renfro said.

Still another incident that seemed to say something about the type of person Paccerelli was had to do with a Cav helicopter that had been shot down in the region. "The helicopter went down at night, and the quick-reaction force was reluctant to go in before dawn. It didn't look good for the downed crew," said Renfro.

"When Paccerelli heard that, he gathered up the only team leaders he could find in the company area at the time and told us to saddle up, that we'd do it. There were just seven or so of us, but for Paccerelli that was enough to go in and search for the survivors. The next problem came when we couldn't get anything but a small Loach helicopter to ferry us into the crash site, which meant that it would have to be three at a time. Paccerelli agreed. He was determined to rescue the crew and went in on the first run and kept the rest of us in reserve in case anything happened.

When he finally got to the crash site, there was nothing he could do. The crew was dead. The enemy was still in the area, but Captain Paccerelli searched anyway. If Paccerelli didn't have the company's respect before the incident, he sure as hell had it afterwards," said Renfro.

Jim McIntyre agreed. "Captain Paccerelli was someone we all respected and admired. He was a Ranger's Ranger," he said. But then, perhaps they were all to be respected for doing a job that few wanted or would do. In a distant war of numbers and nerves, Hotel Company racked up impressive battlefield statistics. By mid-1969 the company had a kill ratio of 44 to one, although it was equally proud of its ability to capture enemy soldiers. In fact, capturing enemy soldiers took priority over killing them so much that the company developed a policy of awarding a three-day in-country R & R to individuals for each enemy soldier brought in alive. On one occasion, after ambushing a North Vietnamese Army patrol, one team leader, armed with only a .45 pistol, chased an ambush survivor down a jungle trail, eventually tackled him, and marched him back to the surprised team.

But, while the LRRPs were making concerted efforts to capture enemy soldiers, the NVA and Viet Cong were doing their best to kill the LRRPs. There had been a rumor of a bounty that the communists placed on the Rangers because of their effective patrols. The rumor of a bounty was never substantiated, but the Viet Cong and North Vietnamese Army feared and respected the small American patrols. While the Viet Cong made the rear areas of South Vietnam unsafe and uncertain for the rear-echelon American and allied units, it was the Ranger units like Hotel Company who, in turn, made the jungle sanctuaries and seemingly remote infiltration routes just as unsafe and uncertain for the communist soldiers who inhabited them. They moved in shadows, quietly and efficiently. Stealth was their watchword and professionalism their standard. When everything went according to plan and the LRRPs were successfully deployed in the field, they proved to be one of the most formidable special operations forces in combat during the Vietnam War. Their primary objective was to gather hard intelligence, and gathering hard intelligence sometimes meant getting within a hand's reach of the enemy in order to learn what he was up to. Hard intelligence eliminated guesswork in strategic planning, and gathering it always meant taking chances.

Operating small patrols deep within enemy-held areas was more than simply a deadly game of cat and mouse. The officers who sent them out knew very well it was like sending one player out against 11 in a grudge-match football game. Unlike the game, though, there would be no time-outs for injuries or for referees to keep things from getting out of hand.

If observation didn't prove to be enough, the patrols would sometimes snatch enemy soldiers from the twisting rain forest trails or ambush small groups of soldiers to get even more tactical information. They would gather what documents and materials they could and quickly disappear into the jungle before the Vietnamese caught on to what was happening and came to investigate. They brought fear to the enemy Vietnamese soldiers and guerrillas utilizing the tactics the Viet Cong had used all too well earlier in the war against the Americans and their allies. While the LRRPs' primary mission was to gather intelligence on enemy operations, a second mission and very real benefit was to unnerve the Vietnamese opponents and make them uneasy in areas of the jungle that were once safe havens.

When it all went according to plan, the LRRPs would carry out their objectives before being extracted at a predesignated pickup zone. Just like clockwork, some said. But time wasn't always on their side, and sometimes, in spite of all the LRRPs' well-laid plans, continuous training, and precautions, the North Vietnamese or Viet Cong would get the upper hand and, in the chaotic moments that followed, the scenario changed, and the hunters became the hunted.

# CHAPTER FOUR

Twilight had given way to darkness, and the rain kept falling, bringing in dark, rumbling clouds that tumbled up and over the countryside. The natural elements that had hidden the North Vietnamese units so well were now working against them. Although the LRRP team's movements had been plotted by the company radio-relay station at a nearby fire support base, Andrus was unable to call for help. The PRC-25, the team's backpack radio, had been shot out of action. Not that it mattered; even with the long whip antenna, the PRC-25 wasn't strong enough to alert the relay station to their situation. The team's only other means of radio contact, the small URC-10, lay in the pack of the dead assistant team leader.

Night positions and situation reports were called in at prescribed times on designated frequencies, using a series of clicks referred to as "breaking squelch," a quiet code used in place of words. This was done both to avoid being overheard in the quiet jungle while one used the radio as well as to make understanding of the team's radio signals difficult. It was well known that the enemy monitored American communications. The RTO would break squelch responding to a series of questions.

"Is everything all right?" The RTO would break squelch once for yes and twice for no. Using similar codes, the team and relay station could respond to almost any situation. "Are you in danger? Do you need help?"

Since everything had been fine at the time of the team's last transmission, the relay station had no reason to believe anything was wrong. At Fire Support Base David, Specialist Don Spaulding waited another 25 minutes or so before attempting to contact the LRRP team. Then, when he hadn't received word from the team after repeated attempts, he contacted the Rangers' tactical operations center in Phuoc Vinh to apprise them of the situation. Better safe than sorry was more than just a saying in Vietnam. It was something your team members and friends lived by.

It wasn't unusual for teams to lose radio contact for hours on end because of the dense rain forests, hills, and draws that hindered radio traffic. Even so, a team had fixed times at which it was to call in its halt locations and to radio in its coordinates and situation reports. Before a helicopter would be dispatched to investigate the situation, Spaulding would try everything he could to raise the missing team. After all, a helicopter hovering over a team to reestablish communication could just as easily lead the enemy to Team 5-2's position.

Concerned but not alarmed, the operations center in Phuoc Vinh and the relay station would give the team every opportunity to come back up on the radio. Spaulding studied his watch intently as another prescribed time for a commo check came and went. The situation didn't look good. Something was wrong, and Spaulding knew it.

A hard rain was beginning to fall over the fire support base, so maybe the weather was interfering with the team's signal, and that was why he couldn't hear the faint calls for a situation report. The volume on the backpack radios was always turned low so only the RTO could hear it, and it was possible that the din of the rain combined with the noises of the jungle had been a temporary distraction. To the relay station and the company's tactical operation center in Phuoc Vinh, the mission seemed to be going according to plan, with only minor radio problems. There was cause for concern, but nothing that could be pointed to with any certainty. If a sixth sense mattered, then the company would have sent out the cavalry immediately, but to do that would take more than just gut-level feelings. In the TOC, they had no way of knowing what had happened or that the three survivors were literally fighting for their lives, desperately trying to hide from the larger enemy force that swarmed over the kill zone and was fanning out to find them.

By 1830 hours, Spaulding reported the negative radio contact to the 1st Brigade's operations officer and then followed up with another situation report to Phuoc Vinh. It was crunch time, and Spaulding knew it. Something was definitely wrong.

A helicopter search was mounted, but the closing weather delayed the attempt. Fog had rolled in to supplement the tumbling rain clouds, and combined, they locked up the Cambodian countryside.

Staring at the cold, black clouds, Spaulding swore quietly. He was originally scheduled to be on the team, but a doctor's order pulled him from the mission. Those were his people out there, and it was more than the cold that made him shiver.

Returning to Fire Support Base David's operations center, he listened for a "situation normal" report that never came. There was nothing on the radio but static.

# CHAPTER FIVE

A Troop, the 1st Squadron of the 9th Cav, was known as Apache Troop rather than by the more common military phonetic designator Alpha. Apache was a troop rather than a company because the 130 or so men in the helicopter-borne unit, like others in the 1st Cavalry Division it belonged to, were considered mounted soldiers rather than infantry. The 1st Cavalry was the first full combat division in Vietnam in 1965. The 1st Cav had more than 500 helicopters, and it had pioneered air mobile tactics in the States as well as in Vietnam. Even the Cav's infantry flew to its objectives before dismounting. Because of the Cav's unique air mobility, the division had taken part in many of the major battles of the war such as the battle of Hue, the relief of the trapped Marines at Khe Sanh in Operation PEGASUS, and the bitter fight for the A Shau Valley.

Within the 1st Air Cavalry there were other Cav squadrons, battalion-size units of light infantry and their own support helicopters. A squadron was composed of company-size helicopter-borne units called troops, which employed a quick-reaction rescue and reconnaissance platoon.

As one of the division's leading reconnaissance squadrons, the 1st of the 9th was considered one of the 1st Cav's elite units in the war, earning the reputation in daily skirmishes.

Apache Troop's roots lay in the history of the famed

Buffalo Soldiers of the 1880s, the all-black cavalry unit led by white officers that carved its niche in the history of the American Southwest, earning for itself the nickname Apache Troop for the enemy it pursued. The Buffalo Soldiers also earned a reputation as one of the boldest cavalry units the world has ever known. To some the title seemed overstated, but to others it was justly deserved, a legacy handed down over the decades.

From its frontier origins through its eventual reorganization and integration into the mainstream Army, Apache Troop always kept close ties to its past. Its horses long since replaced by helicopters in Vietnam, the 1st of the 9th's Skytroopers (as the 1st Cav referred to its members) carried on the link to its past with bold and heroic acts that would continue the legend.

To the bean counters and number crunchers, the 1st Cav accounted for nearly 50 percent of the enemy casualties in the long war, and of those over half were the result of the 1st of the 9th's three air mobile light infantry troops. Since the 1st of the 9th accounted for only 17 percent of the division's strength, the statistics were impressive. However, another very real truth was that the squadron suffered significant losses to achieve its success. It was understood going in that the 1st of the 9th was an outfit for volunteers since reconnaissance meant almost daily skirmishes with the enemy. Ample evidence of constant battle was the zinc chromate primer that visibly marked the numerous small patches and repairs on virtually all of the troops' aircraft. Light metal and Plexiglas seldom stopped enemy rifle fire, let alone armor-piercing rounds.

The 1st of the 9th's effectiveness lay in its mobility and courage. The 21-man ground force each troop employed was considered light infantry. However, its real strength lay in the fact that in addition they usually maintained a six to eight light-helicopter scout platoon, an equal number of

Huey (lift ship) helicopters, and four to six Cobra or Huey B-model gunships for support. The troops were, in fact, self-sufficient.

Each platoon was color coded, the infantry being the Blue force, the scouts the White, and the gunships the Red (for the aerial artillery they represented).

The small Hughes OH-6 scout helicopters, the low birds called Loaches, along with a sleek and deadly Cobra gunship combined to form a Pink Team. Tactically, the scouts would fly low, treetop-level missions to draw enemy fire before pulling pitch as the gunship took over pounding the enemy positions with automatic machine-gun and rocket fire.

In the meantime, the infantry platoon—the Blues—would be ferried in to make contact with the enemy on the ground. The troop's primary objective was reconnaissance; its secondary mission lay in serving as a quick-reaction force (QRF) for other units in need of help within the division.

Whenever any of the Cav's host of helicopters was shot down, the 1st of the 9th took on the task of crew recovery, a rescue force that would try desperately to get to the crew before North Vietnamese Army or Viet Cong patrols. It was common knowledge that the NVA and Viet Cong often ran low on necessary and much needed supplies. Top of the list were medical supplies and surgical kits. It was also understood that what they had, they used for their own because in a war of liberation, victory was the ultimate goal. Humanity would come later, long after the last echoes of the war subsided.

In a literal "race of life," seconds made all the difference as it wasn't uncommon for the enemy to machine-gun the wounded survivors, whether out of retribution for supposed past misdeeds or to serve as a psychological ploy, an object lesson to those who found the crash sites. There would be no second place.

Unlike other infantry or reconnaissance units that sometimes remained in the field for weeks on end, the troop's strategy was to fight quick, decisive battles. Their strengths lay in air mobility and overwhelming firepower, and Apache Troop used them to their advantage, probing here and attacking there, throwing the enemy off balance and keeping him leery of the sound of any approaching helicopter.

As a result, afraid to move in the day and risk discovery, the North Vietnamese Army and Viet Cong battalions began moving at night, making their progress slow and awkward. New strategies were being devised, implemented, and countered as the 61-day raid into Cambodia wore on.

The face of the war was changing once again, and the 1st of the 9th Cav was at the forefront of the change. If the number of pitched chance encounters and sudden firefights the troop found itself involved in was an indicator of the enemy's being thrown off balance, then Apache Troop was doing fine.

Half of the enemy casualty figures tallied were attributed to the 1st Cavalry Division, and the 1st of the 9th figured prominently in the totals.

The Cav fought what some have called a "banker's war"—a seemingly comfortable nine-to-five operation, but seven days a week. While some units would stay out in the jungle for weeks on end, the 1st of the 9th's strategy was to attack and then pull back before the enemy could adjust to the pressure. One lesson that the squadron knew well is how the NVA units and Viet Cong would attack at night, harassing the units in the field and setting up deadly ambushes. The 1st of the 9th avoided such encounters by pulling back to its base camps each night. While most units would search the jungles on the ground, engaging the en-

emy once or twice a month, the 1st of the 9th would encounter almost daily battles, using its air mobility to locate
and frustrate the enemy. Any comfort the men enjoyed in
their bases was lost to the nightly incoming mortar and
rocket attacks. Since the enemy couldn't harass them in the
jungle, he hit them where they lived. Comfort is a relative
term, and the almost daily battles and firefights coupled
with the nightly barrages were something even the grunts
didn't want a part of.

During the raid, the 1st of the 9th was at the forefront of
the action, maneuvering ahead of the enemy and hitting
him before he could regroup and mount an effective
counterattack.

Using stalling or harassing techniques, the Air Cavalry
troops would find the enemy and initiate a fight and then
quickly break off as Air Force fighter strikes, a B-52 bombing mission, or artillery barrages took over the fight.

The 1st of the 9th's casualties were high, and the enemy
was unforgiving in attacks against the scout squadrons. Of
the three new pilots who arrived in February 1969 to serve
with Apache Troop, within four months two would be dead,
and WO-1 Glen Senkowski would be shot down twice.
During his 18 months with the troop, Senkowski's own
ledger would tally a 65-percent casualty rate among the pilots and crews he served with.

Senkowski and the others soon learned that the hunters
could just as easily become the hunted. Lessons were still
being learned, and the growing number of Purple Hearts
and various awards for valor accented the bell curve.

Leading the 1,200 personnel assigned or attached to the
1st of the 9th's various troops or directly under his operational control was a 39-year-old lieutenant colonel from
Oaklawn, Illinois, named Clark A. Burnett.

The six-foot-two-inch, 189-pound Burnett, who was on
his second tour of duty in Vietnam, had a reputation as a

competent professional not only among the higher-ups in
the division but among his men as well. It didn't take long
in combat to see who could do the job, let alone who gave
a damn about those who had to do it. Burnett, whose radio
call sign was Longknife Six, could do the job, and he gave
a damn.

Besides the 850 or so personnel assigned to the squadron, Longknife Six was also responsible for the 118 LRRPs
of Hotel Company, the two dozen combat trackers of the
62d Combat Tracker unit, and 130 aircraft maintenance
troops, give or take.

Burnett had his hands full, and any lessons in leadership
he knew came a day at a time in a war where lessons could
prove painful and costly.

However, five years into the Vietnam War, the 1st Cavalry Division's 1st of the 9th was doing a little teaching of
its own, and among its star instructors was Apache Troop.

# CHAPTER SIX

The Ranger Company's radio-relay personnel at Fire Support Base David began to suspect the worst early on. Infantry LPs, the early-warning two-man listening posts positioned well beyond the small fire support base's perimeter, were reporting heavy small-arms and machine-gun fire as well as explosions, although in the heavy rainfall and jungle, it was difficult to determine the direction the ruckus was coming from. However, with a firefight taking place and Team 5-2 being off the net for several hours, those at the small outpost, especially the Rangers monitoring the team's activities, didn't like the way things were adding up. Specialist Four Spaulding contacted Hotel Company's headquarters to inform them of the latest twist in the situation.

It wasn't unheard of to lose contact with a team for any number of reasons related to difficulties with radio propagation, nor was it uncommon for small, hard-fought battles to be taking place in the AO, the area of operations, but the Rangers weren't taking any chances. Sound carried at night, and what may have sounded to be a few miles away, might very well be taking place at a considerable distance. It wasn't unusual for Air Force planes or Army gunships to be out harassing Charlie either. Still, there was a more than nagging suspicion that something was wrong.

SOP required the brigade to send up a helicopter to fly over the area and try to reestablish contact with the team.

When the Rangers requested one, the brigade gave them a flare ship, and Don Spaulding, flying over the team's last known location and coming up with nothing, no longer had to guess. As far as he was concerned, the team was in trouble. When the helicopter touched down at the fire support base, he quickly reported his findings.

The squadron and the Ranger Company requested a volunteer reaction force to go search for the missing Rangers. When that request was denied, the squadron commander, Lieutenant Colonel Clark Burnett, sent out a request for assistance to Apache Troop, whose men didn't hesitate. While Burnett and the Ranger Company commander, Captain William Carrier, formulated a rescue plan, the pilots of Apache Troop were putting together a volunteer force and a few plans of their own. In the middle of a unit move from the Tay Ninh West base camp to Fire Support Base Buttons in Song Be, Apache Troop's forces were split. But, for a change, that proved to be to their advantage. They'd send out their own overflight from Song Be, although with considerably more punch than just a Huey lift ship. The rest of the force would leave from Tay Ninh and marry up in Cambodia.

As a formal quick-reaction force, and one that was accustomed to on-call operations, Apache Troop put together an operational force consisting of an infantry platoon and supporting Huey helicopter lift ships as well as Cobra attack helicopters for close air support. Quick reaction was Apache Troop's specialty, and one they took seriously. They were around to rescue whoever needed rescuing, putting their lives and skills to the test each time out.

In good weather, they were the home team with a great batting record. In bad weather, they were still good, but the risks of loss climbed dramatically; something not lost on more than a few of the rescue force helicopter pilots who, after taking a good look outside to note the weather, found valid reasons not to leave immediately. The weather was changing again, and the cold, heavy rain was giving way before a closing wall of fog. Dense fog. The kind pilots dreaded. The weather specialists in Song Be said it was a "no go" and there was nothing anyone could do. The cloud cover over Tay Ninh wasn't any better. Someone else said, "Anyone with half a brain could see that much, for Christ's sake."

"What about the LRRPs' sake? We inserted them, so do we just leave them now?" said Warrant Officer Bill McIntosh, studying the critic's face. "What about their sake?" After almost a year of inserting and extracting LRRPs from H Company, the diminutive scout pilot had come to see them as more than unknown faces. He may not have known their names, but Christ! He sure knew their faces!

"We don't know anything's wrong yet? So why rush it?" McIntosh shook his head while another veteran pilot fielded the response.

"That's right, and we don't know yet that everything has gone to shit for them, either. The listening posts reported heavy automatic weapons fire and explosions from the team's direction. The radio relay on David can't get ahold of the team on the radio either. Any way you add it up, it doesn't look or sound good. I say we go anyway. There has to be a ceiling up there somewhere."

"Yeah, well I say we wait," added the critic, "until we know more or at least until the weather breaks. We've already lost two scout crews in Cambodia, that's six of our people shot out of the sky, and we can't afford to lose any more." That was true. Less than two weeks into the invasion, six crew members had died, and several more were wounded or injured. But then, maybe no one knew that better than Bill McIntosh, since those who had been killed were scouts.

After considerable deliberation, it was decided that one

rescue team of volunteers would go up that evening, while the remaining volunteers from Apache Troop would wait until better weather or first light of morning. Flying would be difficult at best, but WO-1 Bill McIntosh of Seattle, Washington, provided the convincing argument. Time was of the essence, he argued. If the LRRP team had been hit, as the indicators suggested, then their one chance might be the presence of a helicopter rescue force overhead, even if it was just a Huey and Cobra gunship team. There had to be a ceiling up there somewhere, and if they could get above it, then they might be the deciding factor for the missing Ranger team. "Hell, if nobody wants to fly with me," he said, "then I'll go up by myself!"

"No, you won't," Warrant Officer Bill Fuller said, grabbing his flight equipment. "You'll need someone to cover your butt. And that, my friend, is me!" An experienced Cobra attack helicopter pilot, Fuller, call sign Apache Two Four, wasn't about to let McIntosh go up alone.

The bravado and point was enough to convince the troop commander, Major William Harris, that it was worth a try. McIntosh was one of his more experienced pilots, and though primarily a scout pilot, McIntosh had considerable experience in lift ships as well. He could fly the ass off the damn thing, and everybody knew it. Sure, he was cocky, but he was good.

The rest of the infantry rescue force comprised the troop's reconnaissance platoon, and while many asked to be part of the first helicopter out, their requests were denied. Restless, the Blues readied their equipment and checked and rechecked their weapons. Because of the nature of the mission, there was no trouble in finding volunteers in Apache Troop or within the Blues Recon Platoon. At least three members of the reconnaissance platoon had served as Rangers with Hotel Company, and others knew members on the missing team. The war had become personal again.

Politics and ideology gave way to anger and frustration at the situation, combined with a genuine willingness to help.

Lieutenant Jack Hugele, of New Orleans, Louisiana, the Blues Platoon leader, had assembled a volunteer force in Tay Ninh, consisting of most of his own platoon and more than a few volunteers from the other platoons in the troop. A team of tracker dogs would also accompany the Blues. Hugele, a Special Forces, Green Beret–qualified officer, felt confident that his people could locate the missing team members. If he could just land at the coordinates of the team's insertion point, he knew he could rely on his point squad to pick up their trail. Dog or no dog. Time and again, the Blues he led had jumped right into the thick of battle, relying on the troop's mobility and firepower and the platoon's recon skills and fighting ability to see them through. But those in the platoon knew that it was also the ability of the lieutenant leading them that made the difference. Hugele, call sign Blue, coordinated the artillery support and the ground action, shoring up the holes while keeping the difficult situations under "reasonable" control.

Hugele was good at his job, but then he had Specialists Jim Braun and Paul Englebretsen, the platoon's best RTOs, to help break him in when he arrived. RTOs did that in combat, and many a smart NCO or young officer was wise to heed their advice. Hugele was anything but dumb, often earning the admiration of his men for making tough decisions quickly after carefully assessing the situation. In some units, higher-ranking officers, flying thousands of feet above the battle, would try to direct the action on the ground. Those young officers who were unsure of themselves might listen to the ranking officer even though the fighting would be obscured from the air because of the distance and the dense overhanging vegetation. Fortunately, Hugele wasn't above telling the occasional interloper just what he could do with his advice; as the officer on the ground, he had the final say, and his say hadn't cost any lives of the men in his command.

The troop's previous commander, Captain Paul "Butch" Funk, had seen that much and trusted the younger officer, and that trust produced results—captured enemy prisoners, caches of weapons and equipment, and in one jungle battle alone, the Blues had managed to work their way inside an occupied enemy battalion bunker complex, leading to one of the major combat actions for the troop, killing 39 North Vietnamese Army soldiers in a desperate day-long pitched battle. It wasn't a firefight either—not a small, sudden skirmish, but a full-scale battle. And the troop had come out on top.

This new mission wouldn't be easy either, yet the quick-reaction force had more volunteers than could be loaded into the available aircraft—aircraft that remained on the ground because of the poor weather. That is, except for the test flight of McIntosh's lift ship and Fuller's attack helicopter.

While neither Hugele nor the platoon liked the delay, there was nothing they could do about it but wait along with the others.

"Who's leading the people from Tay Ninh?" McIntosh asked the tactical operations center radio operator while heading for the flight line.

"Blue Six," the man said, referring to Hugele.

McIntosh nodded. "Good," he said, going through the sandbag-bunker doorway. David was the remote fire support base in Cambodia closest to the LRRP team's last known position. It would be the linkup point for the test flight and rescue force. With nothing more to say, McIntosh headed for the flight line.

At five-foot-six and 127 pounds, Bill McIntosh looked like the Army's first 14-year-old helicopter pilot. With his boyish face and lopsided grin, the diminutive pilot looked like somebody's younger brother playing Army. But the boyish grin was lopsided because a machine-gun bullet had punched through the Plexiglas bubble of his small scout helicopter and entered the left side of his face to lodge in his mouth.

The average scout helicopter pilot would do 500 hours of combat time. If he survived that long. McIntosh, whose radio call sign was One One, already had well over 800, with still a few months to go on his tour of duty. He was pushing his luck, and even he knew it, but with the troop desperately short on experienced pilots, what choice was there? He could have elected to sit out this new mission, but for some reason he couldn't easily define, he decided to volunteer. Everything sensible told him to wait until morning, but to him the only important factor was pulling the LRRPs out as soon as possible. He knew what it was like to be hit and stuck on the ground, waiting, praying, and hoping to God that someone, anyone, would rush out to help him. The operative word here was *rush*. He also understood the overwhelming elation of having the Blues rappel in to pull him and his crew out of danger and save them from certain death.

If you were lucky enough to survive a crash in Vietnam then you also had to survive its aftermath. Just knowing the NVA policy of machine-gunning survivors made each second on the ground something to fear. He had also ferried enough body bags out of crash sites to fully understand the consequences.

Yeah, everything and everyone sensible said to wait, but McIntosh was going anyway. Fuck it. Specialists Dave Harding, the crew chief, and Art Dockter, a veteran door gunner on his six-month extension, were surprised when McIntosh leaned inside their makeshift sleeping area in the helicopter's bay and told them to crank it up. The two crew volunteers had been using the helicopter as sleeping quarters after giving up on trying to keep the rats out of the shelters they were assigned to in Song Be.

When Apache Troop arrived at its new home at Fire Support Base Buttons, the unit had been placed in a new unfinished area of the outpost. In Vietnam, "new" never implied comfort. Luxuries were at a premium, and the troop had to make do in a setting that looked something like a mid-19th-century California gold rush mining camp. It was the kind of camp where simple tents were "uptown"; the majority of the troop lived in what many called "stylish squalor."

The troop's first sergeant, Joe Sparacino, was doing everything he could to make living conditions better, often taking it as a personal affront that his people had to put up with half the crap they did. "It's enough we have to fight this war," he said, arguing for better conditions, "but I'll be damned if we'll do it like beggars or in some rat hole!"

A career soldier, Sparacino was viewed by some as just a crusty old lifer, but he had seen more than his share of combat duty in Korea 18 years earlier when, in just 13 months, he rose from the rank of Private E-1 to that of Master Sergeant E-7 at a time when capable soldiers ran up the rank ladder because of their combat record and efficiency. The price Sparacino paid for the rocketing promotions could be felt on the list he kept of the soldiers under his command who had been killed in action. The penciled names and dates were his reminder that the job was never easy and always at a price that few understood.

Sparacino remembered the Korean War and how he had to carry wounded buddies through hard fighting against tough Chinese regulars only to have to lay them down in mud of a makeshift camp. Years later in Vietnam, the memory was enough to propel him to action. He vowed to take better care of his troops any damn way he could and to keep the list as short as possible. One way was to badger the brass and the engineers to complete the troop's much needed housing and defenses.

The latest unit to arrive on the base, Apache Troop had been assigned makeshift shelters along with an incomplete bunker line perimeter that was, in fact, just a mound of dirt four to six feet high that had been pushed out toward the jungle as a kind of afterthought to the definition of the fire support base. Just one thin line of waist-high barbed wire and five bunkers constituted Apache Troop's perimeter responsibilities. That was a thorn in the side of Joe Sparacino, who saw the shoddy perimeter as a real threat to the security of the troops in his charge. Staying on the backs of those in charge of completing the project was a task he oversaw with keen and grudging interest.

"It's just temporary," they said. "We're doing everything we can."

"Wrong answer!" Sparacino replied. "My people deserve what some of you folks in the rear take for granted. I want the perimeter line finished and their hootches completed. These piss holes they're living in now don't cut it! You understand me?" Sparacino wouldn't take no or anything that amounted to no for an answer.

One of the downsides to the poor living conditions was the rats. Not just rats, but big, cat-size rats that carried as much disdain for the Americans as did the Viet Cong. What finally drove Harding and Dockter to the sanctuary of the helicopter wasn't the number or size of the rats but the way a few of the troop members began picking them off with .45s in their quarters during the middle of the night.

It was the practice with many of Apache Troop's lift ships to remove the side doors, so Harding and Dockter put up ponchos to keep out the driving rain. Of course, when McIntosh stuck his head in and told them to get ready to take the helicopter out, sleeping with the rats began to look like a better proposition. Safer, anyway.

Within minutes, the pilot and copilot were climbing aboard and going through their preflight checks as Ranger Lyle Gayman, the LRRP liaison, joined Dockter and Harding in the bay.

Gayman and Dockter were friends, and the veteran door gunner was surprised to see him. "Any news?" Dockter yelled over the noise as the helicopter cranked up.

Gayman slowly shook his head. "Nothing," he yelled while Dockter, unable to hear what the LRRP had to say, threw up his hands in frustration. "The team's missing," Gayman said. "We think they've been hit!"

When he finally understood what the LRRP had to say, the news hit Dockter with the impact of a punch. He and Harding had inserted Cochrane's team, and they felt very close to it. Dockter had known a number of the Rangers in Hotel Company and had earned awards for heroism for extracting the teams under heavy enemy gunfire, pulling them out of the middle of firefights just as the enemy was closing in. He'd shared their rations, laughed with them over the absurdities of various situations, and felt a kindred relationship with the members of the teams he had inserted and extracted in combat.

"Clear!" Harding said into his headset while Dockter pulled down the makeshift poncho protection and readied his machine gun, checking the linked rounds that overlapped in the ammo box stored beneath his seat.

"We'll find them!" Dockter said to Gayman. "Come on. Let's get our people out!"

As they readied for takeoff, One One rubbed the side of his cheek, thinking back on the hot landing zone where he'd taken the hits several months before. His scout ship, a Hughes OH-6A Loach, and crew—himself, an observer, and the "torque," or door gunner—were skipping over the trees along the border, playing low bird to the Cobra gunship that was acting as the high bird and doing lazy circles thousands of feet in the air. A typical Pink Team, McIntosh's Loach would fly just above the jungle while scouting for signs of the enemy. Then, when some were located, the machine gunner would open up as the observer marked the site with a red smoke grenade for the gunship to roll in on. Red to mark the enemy's position.

Specialist David Ham, of Honolulu, Hawaii, One One's observer, was the first to notice the commo wire running along the dropped ribbon path below. Black and shiny, the wire stood out against the green and brown vegetation. Even from the treetops, the big Hawaiian had no trouble spotting it. Hovering, and then moving sideways to follow the wire, the Loach came to a clearing in the rain forest while radioing in the find and telling the gunship above that it was going to skirt the tree line to the other side of the open field in order to see if they could pick up the wire again.

Flying low over the field was out of the question since the helicopter's only real protection lay in hiding atop the trees. Flying diagonally, or "trim," McIntosh studied the clearing closely, the muscles in his face tightening. Too many times he'd seen helicopters go down from taking the quickest route across an open space—only to be hit with enemy machine-gun fire midway. And too many times the enemy machine-gun rounds had apparently stitched across the aircraft searching for the fuel tank that turned low birds into tumbling fireballs.

McIntosh also knew it was better to fly diagonally since it would throw off the enemy below who was accustomed to leading the helicopters with his machine guns to hit them. If the enemy opened up below, then Mac would pull pitch and take off in an unexpected direction. Sometimes it took more than brass balls to be a good scout pilot. It took a working understanding of enemy tactics and maybe an equal amount of luck.

Skirting the grass-covered opening that was about the size of a football field, McIntosh hovered over the area where he thought the wire would feed back into the jungle bunker complex.

Within minutes Ham spotted it, but Specialist Bill Gannon, the door gunner, noticed something more—a tightly woven bamboo screen that almost blended into the surrounding rain forest was quickly being pushed away. "We got movement!" Gannon yelled, opening up with his M60 machine gun as an enemy .30-caliber machine-gun crew returned fire on the hovering aircraft.

While Gannon was busy with the enemy fighting position, there was no way for him or the others to know it was just part of a fortified North Vietnamese Army bunker complex and that the .30-caliber machine-gun position was only one of several that were occupied. Small-arms fire was coming from myriad directions.

Of the hundreds of machine-gun rounds that flew in their direction, 18 found their mark, slamming into the cockpit. One round went through the clear Plexiglas bubble, bouncing from the roof of the Loach before ricocheting into McIntosh's face, entering just above the jawline and lodging in his mouth. A second round ran up through the bottom of the aircraft but, miraculously, only grazed the pilot's chest, stopping at his helmet. The remaining 16 rounds that hit the scout helicopter took out the machine gun, making it useless. Ham had been hit too, and the low bird was then defenseless.

As his mouth filled up with blood, McIntosh managed to maneuver the helicopter out of the kill zone, all the while fighting for control over the aircraft, which had been severely damaged, and struggling to keep it airborne.

The instruments were gone, and the power was coming in spurts as the veteran scout limped back in the direction of safety, which was still miles away. McIntosh could receive but couldn't transmit, and One One had no way to communicate with the gunship.

After calling in the contact, the Cobra began its turn and run only to lose sight of the low bird. There was nothing remaining but the billowing plume of red smoke indicating where the contact had been initiated. Thinking that the low bird had been shot down, the Cobra called in a downed-helicopter report and told the TOC in Tay Ninh to scramble the Blues as he rolled in to hit the enemy bunker complex.

Meanwhile, One One had Fire Support Base Ike in view and was trying to reach the small jungle outpost. If it went down in the jungle below, no one would know of its location. What was worse, McIntosh had no way of knowing just how badly his crew was hurt. Whenever he snuck quick looks back, all he could see was blood on the face of his door gunner.

Ham was struggling with his own wounds. The big Hawaiian, who had earned a Distinguished Flying Cross for flying a scout helicopter back into base after its pilot had been shot in the chest, was also assessing McIntosh's wounds. Flying a functioning helicopter was challenge enough, but Ham didn't like the idea of having to take over for the pilot in one that was dying. "Put it down! You're hit!" he yelled over the din of the dying helicopter. "Your face. You're bleeding!"

"No," McIntosh said, shaking the suggestion off. "Gotta get to Ike." McIntosh held firmly to his course. If he could put the bird down outside the wire but in the clearing or, better yet, inside, then they'd be okay. Still miles away, the fire support base stood out as a patch of orange clay in the rich green rain forest that surrounded it.

"Ike!" McIntosh had another reason to get to the fire support base. He had to inform the Tay Ninh TOC of the size of the North Vietnamese Army unit in the landing zone because he knew the Blues were going to assault into the

area looking for him and the crew—only they weren't
there. The Blues might lose somebody, and he didn't want
that on his conscience.

In combat, timely information is always at a premium,
and in this instance its value had more meaning.

"Get ready! We're going in!" he yelled. Or thought he
yelled. His speech was slurred from the wounds, blood was
choking him, and periodically, he had to spit to keep from
gagging. The front of his flight suit was awash in his own
blood.

When the grunts on Ike saw the crippled helicopter flying in their direction, they didn't realize what its pilot intended to do, but as that became more evident, they ran to
get out of the way.

As McIntosh headed toward a clearing inside the small
base, the engine seized, and the helicopter gave an ungodly
metallic wail before taking out several radio antennas in the
command bunker and falling beside it. The landing was
rough, and aluminum and Plexiglas helicopters don't
bounce so much as fold. This time was no exception.

Within seconds, the grunts on Ike were clamoring to pull
the crew to safety. Pushing away from an infantry medic after he determined that his crew was okay, the feisty McIntosh made his way to the outpost's commo center and
called in his findings to Tay Ninh, where they were a little
confused that someone identifying himself as One One, but
not really sounding like One One, was calling from a fire
support base, warning them away from the hot landing
zone.

It was only then, when McIntosh was certain that Tay
Ninh understood and believed him, that he let the medics
patch up his wounds.

Earlier on in the year he'd been put in for another award
for saving the lives of an infantry squad that was trapped
by a North Vietnamese Army unit and about to be overrun.

With his door gunner offering support on the ground, McIntosh literally used his helicopter to lower and chop its way down through the trees to get to the beleaguered squad. Then, in three separate flights, he managed to extract the soldiers. To some, McIntosh's actions were gallant, but to the veteran helicopter scout, it was doing something to help others in positions he all too frequently found himself in.

Shot down six times, at times crashing into and through the trees and dense underbrush, McIntosh knew what it was like to be on the receiving end of help. As a pilot and Scout he came to know many of the Ranger teams in Hotel Company, either through inserting them for their five-day missions or as the faces of those who came to the assistance of other scouts who'd been shot down near the Ranger teams' positions. It was common for Rangers and Scouts to buy each other drinks in thanks after such missions. To McIntosh, volunteering as the lead pilot to help search for the missing Rangers was not only part of his job with Apache Troop, but something he knew he had to do. To him, the politics of the war didn't matter as much as the people.

This time One One was flying a larger rescue helicopter, a lift ship, to pull the LRRPs out because if the NVA were laying an ambush, then McIntosh might only get one chance at it. He'd sure as hell try anyway.

Ahead of him, Fuller's sleek Cobra helicopter raced down the flight line and disappeared into the tumbling fog. Lifting the helicopter out of its revetment and watching the other volunteer door gunners and rescuers fill the bay of the lift ship, McIntosh readied for takeoff. Then, as he raced down the airstrip, One One dipped the nose of the Huey lift ship and pulled it over the perimeter barbed wire, gaining altitude as quickly as the aircraft permitted.

Ground level was at 900 feet, and the driving rain and dense clouds obliterated any view over 50. Often less. The cold, thundering blanket before them quickly wrapped itself around the aircraft, and One One knew that the secret of flying in this kind of weather wasn't really flying in it but to get above it rapidly.

Flying IFR, or with instruments only, was virtually flying blind. However, it could be done, and each of Apache Troop's pilots was trained to do it and had done it—though few would readily say they enjoyed it. Many knew that sometimes the fog or monsoon rain clouds hugged the ground in patches or pockets and that if they could get above it, then they could conduct their missions. Go high and get above it. The fog was like a layer of ice over a pond. It was thick and seemingly impenetrable. But as thick as it was, there had to be an upper surface somewhere. Find the top and then you'd skate above it. Easy enough to do provided you didn't run into the back of the lead helicopter, a tree, or a big fucking mountain that lay near the team's last known position.

Finding the missing LRRP team wouldn't be easy, but it could be done. The key was to get into the area where the team had called in its last halt. First, though, McIntosh had to get above the fog. At 1,500 feet, it was steadily churning, and as McIntosh climbed up past 2,000 feet, the fog didn't look as if it would ever end.

# CHAPTER SEVEN

Staff Sergeant Dwight Hancock saw the North Vietnamese soldiers coming out of their foxholes and fighting positions. Seeing the flashlights in their hands and hearing the distinct click of bayonets being fixed, the tall, slender black from San Diego, California, knew it would only be a matter of minutes before the NVA began combing the area looking for the survivors.

While the two wounded LRRPs, Clark and Andrus, hurriedly covered their impromptu hiding place with underbrush and elephant grass, Hancock began obliterating their trail. The night and poor weather conditions were the only breaks the Rangers had, and the three were using them to their full advantage.

Hancock knew that someone had to get word to the fire support base six kilometers away. And since he was the only one who hadn't suffered any injuries, he also knew who it would be.

Informing Clark and Andrus wasn't easy either, but it was necessary. The two LRRPs, armed with only two rifles and 15 magazines between them, would have to remain hidden for as long as it took Hancock to make it to David.

At 1800 hours, armed with only a knife, the uninjured LRRP began to head for help, weaving his way through the wall of jungle. In the distance, the parachute flares from Fire Support Base David provided an eerie guide.

Crawling rapidly and covering his tracks, Hancock made it down a long hill before rising to a running crouch, heading north to a jungle stream that could conceal his path.

He eased into the warm, slow, muddy water, crossing it quietly. When he emerged on the opposite bank, he felt what he at first thought were slimy chunks of mud clinging to his exposed flesh. But it wasn't mud. Dozens of leeches clung to his skin, sucking out the blood.

In a panic, he quickly knocked off those he could see, then he regained his composure and once again began to work his way toward the small American outpost in the distance. He was lost in the fog, but the sound of the outgoing artillery rounds provided him with a direction. A short time later, he discovered a second stream and as he started to work his way across it, he paused when he heard voices directly ahead of him. Vietnamese voices.

Stopping midstream his eyes began to distinguish between the shadows of the jungle and those of the North Vietnamese soldiers. From his position, he could make out 20 to 25 North Vietnamese soldiers resting on the near bank. The noise from their conversation hid the sounds the LRRP had made coming to the stream.

Very carefully, he turned downstream, and with all the caution he could muster, he quietly moved away from the enemy encampment. A few hundred yards farther away, he slipped into the water, treading his way across as the leeches took hold. This time, though, knowing the leeches would probably be the least of his problems, he remained surprisingly calm.

# CHAPTER EIGHT

Glen Senkowski rubbed his tired eyes and yawned. Inside the Apache Troop tactical operations center, the TOC, the radio traffic was minimal, and besides the constant drone of the generators that kept the radios operating, there wasn't much going on in the province, let alone in neighboring Cambodia.

As a veteran slick pilot, Senkowski was on strip alert, that is, basically, it was his turn at bat. If the Ranger team needed to be extracted, then it would be his job and the job of his UH-1H helicopter crew to pull the team out. The job was just another of the tasks rotated among the Huey lift-ship pilots in the troop.

Even though the Ranger company had its own relay stations, the Apache Troop tactical operations center monitored the Rangers' radio traffic, too. Since they inserted the teams in the region and extracted them at the end of their five-day patrols behind the enemy lines, the pilots listened in on the brigade frequency monitoring the party line with more than casual interest.

Most of the time, inserting the LRRPs was easy. After the team leader made his overflight of the proposed landing zone and the pilot committed it to map and memory, the helicopter would return to Tay Ninh, pick up the rest of the LRRPs, and then fly in for the real thing.

Since the jungles in III Corps were so vast and thick, the

enemy couldn't monitor every potential landing zone. Besides, the helicopters were only on the ground for ten seconds or so. Most of the time, they would barely touch down before the five Rangers had scrambled out of the helicopter cargo area and hurried into the edge of the rain forest. Then, the lone helicopter would dip its nose and get the hell out of the area.

High above, an accompanying Cobra gunship helicopter would wait and watch over the action or lack of it. Most of the time, things went like clockwork. Most of the time.

Senkowski checked his watch wondering how long the mess tent would stay open. Once the Ranger relay made contact with Team 5-2, he'd maybe check with the officer on duty to find out if he could make a run over to the chow hall, quickly grab something, and return with it to the TOC. C rations were okay, but real meat on bread sounded better. The chief warrant officer was just about to do that when he heard the Ranger relay station run a commo check over the radio again. An hour earlier, the call had gone unanswered, which could've meant any one of a number of things. This new request, though, seemed more suspect.

"Talon Five Two. Talon Five Two. Radio check. Over." The call was followed by a radio breaking squelch and the dead air that always reminded Senkowski of the sound TVs made when you were between channels. "Talon Five Two. Talon Five Two. Radio Check. Over," the relay station called again, still with no response.

Several long moments followed, and the caller's bored request became more serious. Heads in the TOC turned toward the radio that was tuned to the Ranger frequency. Extended loss of radio transmission was always cause for concern. Being out of radio contact for a short while wasn't unusual, but the long spells were something else.

"Maybe it's the weather," Specialist Jim Braun said, turning to Senkowski. A veteran radio-telephone operator, the big man was offering the benefit of the doubt, or perhaps a prayer. Outside, the light rain was turning to a heavy downpour. Braun knew that major weather fronts didn't do much to help radio transmissions. A former infantry radioman with the Blues Platoon, a "Blue India" (i.e., the recon platoon leader's main radioman), Braun was an obvious choice to work the TOC when his time in country was winding down. In fact, he was one of just a number of men then working the TOC in shifts, veterans of the troop whose tours were also quickly winding down. The specialist's face displayed more worry than his tone had implied.

"I hope so." Senkowski, like Braun, was beginning to think there was something more to the silence than just bad radio conditions, but he didn't want to give voice to his fear. Ten minutes later, Senkowski forgot his hunger as the Ranger relay station tried once again to establish contact with the missing patrol. And again came up short. Still later, when the relay station again failed to make radio contact, the adrenaline began to surge through Senkowski's body, the unwitting response to a feeling in his gut. "I don't think it's the weather," Senkowski said reluctantly.

Braun, the big man, nodded in agreement. "Me neither," he said. In March of the previous year, Chief Warrant Officer Senkowski had received the Distinguished Flying Cross for extracting another LRRP team that was engaged in a vicious firefight with a North Vietnamese Army unit they had ambushed earlier. After blowing their claymore antipersonnel mines on what they thought was a small patrol, the LRRPs had soon discovered it was actually the point element for a much larger enemy force.

Grabbing the maps and papers the dead enemy soldiers had in their possession, the Rangers quickly tried to slip back into the jungle before the rest of the enemy force could figure out what had happened. The Rangers had almost made good their escape when the enemy picked up their trail and began to close on the five Americans. When the team called for a running extraction, Senkowski and his crew scrambled out to the designated pickup zone. Trouble was, when they arrived the Rangers were pinned down, dead enemy soldiers all around them, and the pickup zone was firefight hot. The accompanying gunship made a protective pass over the enemy positions, hammering them with Gatling-gun fire and rockets, as Senkowski brought the Huey in for the pickup. Touching down in the middle of an ongoing battle was about as easy as someone's trying to continue the barbecue after knocking over a nearby hornet's nest. Only the stings from the enemy machine guns were considerably more damaging.

Specialist Five Art Dockter, Senkowski's crew chief, was working the jungle tree line with his M60 machine gun, covering the LRRPs' escape and yelling for them to hurry. Before the first LRRP had jumped aboard and turned back to provide protective fire for the others, the incoming enemy rounds were stitching their way across the aircraft's tail boom and working toward the cockpit.

"Shit!" Senkowski yelled as the electrical system went out—along with the oil cooler. Still, he held the helicopter in place as the rest of the team hurried to the aircraft. "Come on! Come on! Come on!" he was saying, more to himself than to the others. A veteran pilot who, during his 15 months in country, had aircraft take hits on five separate occasions, Glen Senkowski had pushed his luck one too many times, and in combat the house always favored the enemy.

As two of the LRRPs reached out and literally yanked the last team member aboard, Senkowski dipped the nose of the aircraft for a running start. Then, to his surprise and relief, the aircraft shuddered but lifted out of the hot landing zone as the North Vietnamese Army soldiers came running out of their firing positions and tried without success to shoot down the damaged helicopter. Later, in Tay Ninh, the Ranger team leader waited by the flight line for Senkowski to park the aircraft. As other pilots and members of the troop gathered around to look at the many hits the slick had taken, the Ranger team leader walked over to him and held his hand out. "Here, sir," the LRRP said as he handed Senkowski one of the company's wooden-nickel tokens. "It isn't much for what you did, but I'd like you to have it anyway." The tokens were left by the Rangers at the site of their ambushes as calling cards for the enemy; the coins also served as gifts to those the LRRPs thought worthy of their respect. You didn't get one easily, and while the face value meant nothing at all, their significance was more far-reaching.

"Thanks," the Michigan native said, staring at the wooden coin and genuinely pleased. "But I think I need a drink more, about now."

The LRRP laughed and said he'd be glad to do the buying. Staring back at the bullet-riddled helicopter, the LRRP realized he needed a stiff one, too.

A week or so afterward, Senkowski had been awarded the Distinguished Flying Cross for valor. Now, waiting in the TOC and fidgeting as he stood by the radio, he thought about the rescue mission, the many bullet holes in his aircraft, the Distinguished Flying Cross, and something about not taking any wooden nickels.

An hour later, there had still been no contact with the missing Ranger team, and as the long night wore on without radio contact, the suspicion that the missing LRRPs were in trouble was all but confirmed. A plan was being formulated to attempt a rescue in the early morning, and the lift ships were being readied by their crews while the ground rescue force was being gathered. Senkowski knew he wouldn't be part of the rescue attempt, and he wasn't asked. The rescue force would consist of only the few aircraft the troop had available, and they'd need fresh pilots. Senkowski and the others in the TOC were told to stand by. He'd have to sit on the sidelines, and like any defensive player studying the scoreboard late in a crucial game, he probably hoped the offense could make something happen. And, too, maybe a small part of him was secretly glad he wouldn't have to be sent back in to take any more hits. He'd go if he was asked or if he was needed, but he wouldn't relish it. Earning a wooden nickel cost more than most people could ever comprehend, and he had a suspicion more of them would be handed out after this new mission. To anyone lucky enough to survive.

# CHAPTER NINE

At 3,000 feet, the rain diminished as predicted, but not the intense cloud cover or the hammering turbulence. But McIntosh, call sign One One, was wrestling with a new set of problems. The kind of problems that made the cold, wet, and bumpy ride more than just routine.

A note tacked up in the tactical operations center, the TOC, back in Tay Ninh read: When you're up to your ass in alligators, it's hard to remember that your assignment is to empty the swamp.

Apache One One was up to his ass in alligators. The helicopter's FM and UHF radios were out, and One One was unable to contact the gunship that accompanied him, let alone the 1st of the 9th TOC that was overseeing the operation and the rescue attempt. They'd also lost contact with the radio-relay people in Song Be at Apache Troop's new home, Fire Support Base Buttons, not to mention any and everyone else. Great, thought One One. We're flying alone.

Flying on instruments was tough, even with the radios. The accompanying gunship could very well be within a few feet of the aircraft, and in the dense fog, a collision wasn't out of the gloomy picture either. Without the aircraft's instruments, the odds for the rescue attempt dropped considerably, not to mention the odds for their own survival.

To complicate matters, jarred by the thunder and

turbulence and maybe one too many hard landings, the instrument panel was acting up.

The Huey lift ship was the troop's and division's workhorse helicopter, and it could take quite a beating. Although the maintenance sections sometimes worked miracles getting them patched up and flying, the combat wear and tear was taking its toll.

One One was flying deaf and blind and, like Helen Keller, he relied heavily upon feel, on touch, as he maneuvered the helicopter through the realm of the lost.

He could not tell where the gunship was, and now finding the missing LRRP team became secondary to his aircraft's survival. In this region, running into a mountain wasn't out of the question.

His tactical map of the Vietnamese-Cambodian border area showed peaks from 900 to 3,000 feet. Although the map was useless in the fog and at night, it did warn him of the natural dangers he faced in addition to the more obvious man-made variety.

Taking the helicopter up steadily, McIntosh climbed to pull out of the fog and cloud cover. There had to be a ceiling up there somewhere. At 11,000 feet, he finally found it.

In the open bay, Harding, the crew chief; Art Dockter, the experienced door gunner; and the Ranger company's Apache Troop contact man, Lyle Gayman, were fighting to stay warm. Since the helicopter's doors had been removed for the quick exits and the mobility the Cav prided itself on, the wind, heavy rain, and now biting fog were combining to make it a miserable flight.

Technically, the Huey was rated to go to 10,000 feet, although nobody recommended it. McIntosh had a valid reason to push it. Three in fact.

Any other pilot might have decided to put the aircraft down and wait out the bad weather, but that tactic usually applied to daylight operations. Never at night.

The fog and cloud curtain didn't make landing all that easy, as well as the notion of perhaps landing in the lap of an enemy eager to get back at any American aircraft crew, let alone one belonging to the 1st of the 9th, which had led the attack. So One One held firm to the only logical choice—climb high enough to see where the hell you're going.

"Try the VHF," McIntosh said to his copilot, who rogered the request, then made the change. Seconds later, hoping for any response at all, McIntosh began calling to any aircraft in the area. As he was doing that, McIntosh couldn't help but recall a joke he had heard. Something about a man standing on the edge of Echo Canyon, only to lean over the side and yell, "Helllllooooo!" His surprise at the booming echo made him teeter and fall. And as he was falling into the seemingly bottomless chasm, he miraculously reached out and grabbed a lone branch growing on the face of the cliff.

Pulling himself up with his other hand, he hugged the branch for dear life. "Is ... is there anyone there?" he called back up the cliff. "Please? Is anyone there?"

For what seemed like an eternity, there was no response, and then, finally, a voice called back. "This is God. Trust me. Let go."

The tiring man thought it over a few seconds, and then called out a second time. "Is anyone else there?"

McIntosh knew that in any emergency situation a reasonable answer was worth waiting for.

"Apache One One to any station. Mayday! I say again, Mayday!"

"Apache One One," an almost casual voice answered over the headset. "This is Big Brother. How can we help?" The response was from a surprised Air Force B-52 Bomber returning to Thailand after a bombing mission. The bomber's pilot was wondering what the helicopter was doing up so high and asked as much.

Grinning, McIntosh stated his problem and position and had the B-52 bring the gunship and troop TOC on line with the VHF frequency.

What the hell? A party line was better than no phone at all. Given the circumstances, who cared who was listening in anyway? Even if the enemy far below had an eavesdropping capability, he wouldn't be able to make much sense of the conversation anyway. The enemy intercept operators might have been skilled in English and technical military terms, but the pilots used slang and swear words to punctuate points or convey simple messages. Big Brother wasn't the bomber's call sign, it was the Air Force pilot's way of letting the Army helicopter know that someone was there for him.

It was no secret that some pilots resorted to "team talk," a kind of slang in which a particular phrase or term was used only in the unit involved. Aircrews lived in a world of their own, and in this war, they just as often died there as well.

Once contact was reestablished, some of the worry receded, especially for First Sergeant Sparacino, who was monitoring the radio traffic. Sparacino had flown with McIntosh on one special operation when the hotshot pilot had to put down in the middle of the enemy-infested jungle when their helicopter malfunctioned.

The mishap didn't seem to bother McIntosh, who took that particular Mayday with indifference. Sparacino knew otherwise, but chalked it up to McIntosh's combat experience. Or brass balls. The kid had them. If he wasn't the troop's gutsiest and craziest pilot, then at least he was in the running!

First Sergeant Sparacino made an audible sigh of relief when One One's voice came over the TOC's radio. At least he wouldn't have to add McIntosh's name and those of the others to his growing list.

Now, it was just a matter of available fuel and the poor visibility.

"Abort the mission and turn around," the TOC said, informing One One of the command decision.

"We still have time," McIntosh replied, checking his gauges and hoping they were correct. As the readings alternated between the real and the surreal, One One and his copilot snatched quick readings. The haunting question was, when they seemed to be working, were they correct?

"Negative, One One. The weather's closing. Turn around, and the tower will bring you in. You've just enough flight time to get back. Six says you can try again at first light."

McIntosh wanted to argue but knew the TOC was right. "Come on back on my heading," the tower replied while McIntosh reluctantly complied.

"You think we'll run out of fuel?" his copilot asked the veteran scout. A touch of worry was evident in his voice as he studied the instrument panel.

"Naw. We're fine!" One One laughed. He didn't have the heart to tell the new guy he was more worried about running into a mountain on their way back than running out of fuel. The fog had a way of hiding the obvious.

# CHAPTER TEN

Cold and tired, Hancock worked his way through the sulking rain forest, past the pockets of enemy soldiers, and headed toward Fire Support Base David. He'd lost track of time.

His adrenaline was spent, and he moved on what little energy he had left. The parachute flares from the remote outpost provided him with a ghostly guide as they slowly singsonged their way to the jungle's floor before burning out in a final burst of pale magnesium light. That night, moving through the rain forest was like trying to cross an obstacle course in the dark while someone set off a series of unsynchronized flashbulbs. Tree limbs and shadows became enemy soldiers, until the short bursts of light unexpectedly revealed real soldiers—silhouetted individuals or groups crouched, stooped, waiting in the dark. Their sudden appearance startled the Ranger, who moved away as stealthily as he could.

The reports of the fire support base's outgoing artillery rounds were growing louder, so Hancock knew he couldn't be very far from the small base. The trouble was that he didn't know who or what might lie between his position and the outpost. He had encountered enemy patrols along the way, avoiding some and being chased by others, but he had kept pushing forward. And as if the enemy wasn't dangerous enough, at one point, Hancock blundered across a small herd of water buffalo. At 900 to 1,200 pounds each, the beasts were normally placid with the Vietnamese but seemed to be agitated by the presence of Americans. Water buffalo had been known to ram tanks and jeeps. Never mind the number of unsuspecting GIs they had chased. Hancock slipped in among the small herd before moving back into the tree line and relative safety.

The night worked to the Ranger's advantage because while the enemy didn't expect to see a lone American soldier walking through the rain forest, Hancock expected to find the enemy everywhere. His caution was more than good sense, and its benefits were making themselves evident with each new threat or potential threat he avoided.

As his eyes grew accustomed to the ever-changing pitch-darkness of the jungle, Hancock advanced on David, carefully picking his way through the underbrush. Sound carried at night, and any unusual sound, such as a footfall on a twig, might very well get him killed.

Eventually, Hancock ran across one of the base's two-man listening posts—an advance warning position manned by grunts from FSB David—and he thought better of trying to advance to them. Men on LP duty were frequently very trigger-happy. Skirting the position, Hancock moved even more cautiously.

A few hundred yards off of Fire Support Base David, Hancock came to an abrupt stop. It suddenly came to him that he couldn't just walk up to the barbed-wire perimeter any more than he could have just walked up to the two men in the LP. The grunts in their fighting positions on the other side of the wire would be just as nervous and on edge as those on the LP, waiting and watching for any new signs of an enemy ground probe. There was the additional problem that he couldn't very well yell for help either because that would probably attract enemy fire to him. And what about trip-wired booby traps or land mines?

In the midst of Hancock's ruminations, the sound of a rifle shot carried through the Cambodian night despite the weather. Even though the forests and the rolling hills it covered had muffled it somewhat, the sound was clear and ringing. Minutes later, the second followed, and even before the third echoed to his location, there was no doubt what was going on. The NVA were trying to flush out the remaining Rangers by firing single shots into likely hiding places. It was an old tactic, but one that still worked despite its age. Individual enemy soldiers would follow the direction their escaping opponents had taken and find several likely hiding sites. Then, waiting until the rest of his unit was in position, the NVA soldier would fire a round in the area, hoping to either hit an enemy soldier or draw return fire. If no one cried out or nothing happened, the soldier would find another site and repeat the process until the Americans were located. Once found, the fight would begin again. Like hunting quail, the enemy first had to flush out the birds. Then he'd carefully take aim and fire. With most of their equipment and all of their rucksacks still in the ambush site, the Rangers could do little else but hide, hold on, and hope that Hancock had somehow gotten through. But would he get through in time? The enemy was making no attempt to mask or mute his search. He wanted the Americans to fire, and when they did, they would be killed. Flushed out. But that would come later. For now, the spaced individual shots that rang out were the bugle sounding the hunt was on.

Moving more cautiously now as the fire support base came into view, Hancock found a tattered white parachute from an expended flare and hoped it would be enough to keep the grunts from firing.

Settling down to his own nightmare, walking through the cold, wet scrub brush while clutching the tiny parachute, Staff Sergeant Dwight Hancock listened to the volume of the war, the boom of outgoing, punctuated by the distinct sounds of single shots. Jarred by the activity, he kept on walking, hoping he'd be in time to save the others. To some, his trek might have looked like a flight for his own life, but Hancock knew he was running to save the others, too. Time was everything, and since he couldn't carry the others back, he'd get to David as fast as he could to increase their chances of survival.

It wasn't enough just to escape and evade. Those were his team members out there, and screw what anybody thought—their only chance to survive fell on his shoulders, and as he moved through the rain-soaked jungle, he knew he couldn't let them down.

# CHAPTER ELEVEN

Specialist Four Francis Anthony Cortez was a short-timer, a double-digit midget, which meant that the six-one, 175-pound infantryman had less than a hundred days left to go on his tour of duty in country. The proverbial downhill slide and an Apache Troop short-timer.

Seventy days, to be specific, and Tony was looking forward to going home. As a former 60 gunner with the Blues Recon Platoon—a machine gunner—he had seen his share of combat and, as a result, had earned a rear-area job from the grateful troop, courtesy of First Sergeant Sparacino whose unofficial official policy meant looking after his people.

While most officers and unit medics did a six-month combat tour, the average enlisted man was expected to do a full year. In Apache Troop, the unofficial policy was to look after the enlisted men and to reward them for exceptional service. One method came in the form of rear-area or base camp jobs, which allowed the enlisted man to climb down gradually from his combat edge before returning home.

Cortez had been on edge, too. During his tour he had seen and taken part in it all—everything from sudden, arm's-length jungle battles to the defense of fire support bases that the North Vietnamese had tried their damnedest to overrun. On one such miserable occasion, worn and weary after a long night of fighting, he took in the aftermath of an NVA sapper's damage—the NVA soldiers' best infiltrators who, preceding predawn attacks, slipped silently through the perimeter's barbed-wire defenses, set and planted their explosives, and then waited for them to blow so the rest of the attacking enemy force could charge through the opening.

Guard bunkers near his own were blown inside out, and charred, splintered bits and pieces of soldiers were left in the wake of the attack before the Americans finally drove the assault force out of the perimeter.

Cortez had been on countless helicopter rescue missions, too, racing to save downed aircrews from the Viet Cong and NVA soldiers. The enemy knew he could expect a nearly instantaneous reaction to a downed aircraft, so he was determined to beat the rescuers to the crash site.

In this race to save lives, Apache Troop was more than just a contender. Most of the time, Apache Troop beat the enemy in the deadly race, its OH-6A scout helicopters hovering over and guarding the crash site with machine-gun fire until the Blues Platoon could work through the thick foliage, reach the crash site, and secure a makeshift perimeter. Then, the survivors were pulled from the tangled wreckage by Cortez and the others as the platoon set up a medevac extraction for the injured or wounded.

Occasionally, the scout helicopters and the NVA would arrive at the same time, then battle for control of the crash site. The NVA were generally very tenacious because they knew the helicopters could only remain on station for so long before having to return to base for fuel.

It was at times like those when the small aluminum and Plexiglas scout helicopters took hits of their own, falling back while the Blues took over on the ground. And it was at times like those that Cortez's ability with the machine gun came into play, along with that of Specialist Four

Duane Bloor of Hillsboro, Wisconsin, the second machine gunner in the platoon. Together they'd drive the enemy back with deft interlocking fire as the rest of the platoon secured the area and helped with small-arms fire.

The 5.56mm round of the infantryman's M16 tumbled and changed trajectory when it hit a branch between the infantryman and his intended target; the larger M60 machine-gun round and its impressive range cut through the dense underbrush, seeking out soft targets and making it difficult for the enemy to keep up a sustained attack, let alone overrun an American position.

Cortez and Bloor were good, and their ability often became the pivotal point in sudden firefights. A former boxer, Cortez worked the light machine gun the way he jabbed. Short, quick bursts kept the opponents reeling while Bloor's raking fire sent them running. The combination proved effective. After a while, a third machine gunner was added to the Blues. Although the platoon's table of organization showed only one actual position for the machine gun, the platoon actually carried two or more, salvaging the weapons from destroyed helicopters and giving the 17- to 21-man platoon improved firepower.

Since the NVA were well aware of standard American tactics and deployment in the field, they were often confused by the unusually high volume of machine-gun fire the platoon was able to produce. Going up against company-size enemy elements, the Blues could do more than just hold their own.

However, there were times when no matter how fast the Blues responded to the downed aircraft siren that sent them scrambling for the flight line and the first helicopter out, no matter how fast the scouts or UH-1H lift ships flew to get to the crash sites and offered fire support, the enemy beat them there.

The NVA seldom took prisoners from the downed aircraft, choosing instead to kill whoever had been fortunate or unfortunate enough to have survived the crash. Cortez had seen that, too.

Bullet-riddled bodies still trapped in the tangled, burning wreckage were sometimes all that the platoon found. Such occasions were a grim warning and reminder to Apache Troop, one that registered hard on the rescue force and especially on Cortez.

Since the Blues were basically a helicopter unit, it wasn't uncommon for the rescue force to be going after one of its own aircraft. "You don't forget seeing your friends that way," the Azusa, California, resident said to a young buck sergeant everybody called the Wise Guy. "It's something that stays with you, something that makes you push harder the next time out. If for no other reason than for your own peace of mind."

The Wise Guy nodded over a beer. Usually a smart-ass, the Wise Guy withheld his comments, knowing that time and place were everything and that the war wasn't always won by a punch line.

Cortez's reasoning seemed to motivate the rest of the platoon as well. While many of the political justifications of the war didn't sit well with a lot of the soldiers in Vietnam that late in the war, the one thing that was well understood is that you fought for your buddies; you protected your own. That was something they could all cling to when the politics, theories, and bullshit reasons fell victim to the zipping sound of a closing body bag.

In 70 days, Tony could leave the war behind him. But when Sergeant Robert Edward Beal, a former LRRP/Ranger with Hotel Company and one of the two point men for the Apache Troop Blues, went looking for volunteers to rescue the missing Ranger team, Cortez knew he'd volunteer again for the very same reasons he was fighting the war.

"When do we go?" was all he said after Beal explained the situation. Although the platoon had already replaced him with another machine gunner, Cortez settled for an M16 and a place with the point squad.

"When the weather breaks," Beal replied. "Have your weapon and web gear ready on the flight line in 15 minutes."

Cortez nodded. So much for a safe, rear-area job. Cortez laughed to himself, thinking that maybe the 70 days didn't matter as much as he'd thought they would. Being a short-timer in a war didn't guarantee anything. Of course, being a volunteer didn't help his chances of survival either.

"What do you think? Think they're still alive?"

"I hope so," Beal said. He'd known the missing LRRP/ Ranger team leader and several members of the team. The war had a way of becoming very small and visceral. "Either way, it'll be dangerous."

"What do you mean 'either way'?" Cortez asked.

"Well, if they're dead, then the NVA will probably wait to see who comes looking for them. Either that or they just leave their bodies for us to find."

"But you don't think so," Cortez said, guessing Beal's thoughts.

"No, I don't," the North Carolinian said. "Dead or alive, I think the NVA will use them as bait to draw us in before they spring another ambush."

"Either way, we're going in. We can't leave them. We don't leave our people behind, right?"

Beal nodded. "See you on the flight line in 15 minutes," he said as he left to gather the rest of the volunteers.

Cortez nodded solemnly, turning back and readying his equipment. There was nothing else to say. Beal was right. Cortez didn't much appreciate the idea of being bait, but he hated the notion of leaving the LRRPs alone to fend for themselves even more.

The knock on the hootch door and the smiling face of the Wise Guy momentarily distracted Cortez from thought of the missing Rangers.

"Figured you'd be going," the Wise Guy said, watching Cortez tape a survival knife to the shoulder straps of his web gear.

"Look who's talking," the Californian said, staring at the buck sergeant who was armed to the teeth; teeth that were usually seen through a sarcastic smile. But the smile was a temporary facade; it wouldn't last because Cortez knew that once the Wise Guy boarded the lead helicopter, he was all business. "I thought you had a rear-area job, too?"

"I do," the Wise Guy replied. "It'll still be waiting for me when I get back, along with yours." Then, changing the subject, the Wise Guy echoed Sergeant Beal's concern. "You scared at all?"

"Nope. You?" Cortez said, putting on his web gear and checking his work to make sure the knife was accessible.

"Nope," the Wise Guy replied, handing Cortez his rifle. "You lying, too?" he added.

"Yeah."

"Me, too. Ain't reality a bitch?"

"You're crazy, you know that?"

The Wise Guy nodded and smiled. "Makes it easier to do the job at times. You want to know what else I think is a bitch?"

"What?"

The expression on the face of the Wise Guy turned sour. "Doesn't it seem odd to you that we're flying 50 or so miles in to pull these guys out when there's another unit closer to them?"

Cortez paused, studying the Wise Guy. "Yeah, I guess it does. What's up?"

The Wise Guy shrugged. "Who knows? Sounds like somebody's being chickenshit. I heard Colonel Burnett's pissed about it, too. Maybe somebody close by thinks it's too dangerous to send their people."

"Which means if we don't go in for them, then nobody else will."

"Looks that way, Tony."

Cortez shook his head and grabbed his web gear. "Screw 'em. Let's go find our people."

Bait or no bait, the hook was set. Again.

# CHAPTER TWELVE

"No go," Lieutenant Hugele said to the assembled volunteer force after coming from the troop TOC and hearing that both helicopters were on their way back. His voice matched the bleak predawn morning. Outside, the overhanging fog had fallen to a 30-foot ceiling, giving Fire Support Base Buttons a surreal tone. Ghostlike grays danced and twirled to an eternal rhythm.

"The helicopters couldn't make it to David, and David's taking incoming anyway," the lieutenant said, staring at the crestfallen faces. Adrenaline could only carry the men so far, and at well after midnight, the restlessness was a sign of strain. The roller coaster of emotion and the frustration of waiting was getting old. The volunteer ground force tried to make themselves comfortable, and a few succeeded. The platoon command post for the Blues was early *Grapes of Wrath*—a makeshift Hooverville slum where wooden crates and boxes made up most of the rough-hewn furniture: an odd mix of olive-drab military coloring and unvarnished light wood. A card table bore the nomenclature numbers of the gunship rockets it had once held, and the chairs were an odd mix of jeep seats and upended ammo crates.

Slumlike it may have been, but it was also familiar and, considering the time and locale, comfortable. The volunteers settled in with few complaints or whining. The CP was home this side of Oz in a land where everyone knew there were no such things as flying monkeys, but where other nasty surprises lay in wait to jump out and grab you.

"So we wait. When it clears we go?" Staff Sergeant Robert Payton Burrows said. The way he said it, the words were more a statement of fact than a question. Burrows, who was working as the assistant platoon sergeant, was one of the platoon's few professional soldiers, one of the few lifers among the group. The platoon sergeant, a sergeant first class (SFC) named Kenneth Yeisley, was another. But Burrows was unique because he was the platoon's only real multi-lifer in the group since he believed he was a reincarnated warrior whose past lives included tours of duty with Patton at the Bulge and a life or two with the legions of Rome.

A skilled infantryman and avid historian, the tall, hulking staff sergeant relished the war in a way few had. Burrows liked the fighting, liked the whole concept and notion of war. He had chosen to return to Vietnam for another tour after going home on a 30-day leave and finding little there to his liking.

"Here you have a purpose," he said to another squad leader after returning from the States. "Back in the World, they could care less about what we're trying to do. They're so fucked up, they don't even know what they're doing! Here, we got purpose."

"Like what? Bomb these little fucks back into the Stone Age?" the squad leader asked. He was a 19-year-old buck sergeant whom Burrows hadn't quite pigeonholed yet. Although Burrows knew the squad leader liked to walk point, the fellow had a nasty habit of being, well, a smart-ass. A real wise guy.

"No!" protested the staff sergeant. "Stopping the spread of communism!"

"Oh yeah, I forgot. We're the last outpost of freedom. Never mind that these people have been fighting each other for, oh, I dunno, 2,000 years, or that the Viet Minh were our allies during World War II against the Japanese."

"So, what are you saying?" Burrows asked ominously.

"I'm saying I don't have a purpose for being here other than doing my time and going home afterward. I don't give a shit about politics, but it seems that somebody lied to somebody. I'm saying I don't understand half of the reasons why we're here, and the more of this place I see, the less I'm convinced of the reasons anybody tells me. In short, I'm telling you I don't give a rat's ass about a domino theory when the two biggest communist governments, the Soviet Union and Red China, not only don't see eye to eye, but they hate each other's guts. Seems like nationalism to me hiding behind some bullshit about socialist brotherhood. I'm telling you I hate seeing our people die for a cause the people back home don't give a damn about anyway. So, have I left anything out that might make you think I like it here?"

The Wise Guy's response caught the professional soldier off guard, and Burrows waited a few moments before he finished sizing the kid up. "You and James Dean, rebels without a cause."

The squad leader shook his head. "Yeah, and you and Richard Nixon, rebels without a clue. No. I once read somewhere how female flying ants mate in the air, and then afterward they rip their wings off and stay on the ground."

"What does that have to do with anything?"

"Simple. Like the freshly screwed ant, I don't give a flying fuck about what's happening here. My cause is to do my job and go home when my tour's done, and to see that the people in my squad make it home, too, with as few injuries as possible. Other than that, my vision isn't as clear as yours."

"What we're doing here is right!" Burrows said. He was

slightly more than pissed, and the thick, cord-like veins were beginning to jump in his neck.

The Wise Guy shrugged and threw his hands up. "Right or wrong doesn't matter. We're here," he said, thinking he was finished blowing off steam.

But Burrows wasn't about to let the argument end, which only escalated the argument. Neither of the two NCOs gave ground—not the squad leader, whom the veteran staff sergeant knew to be a competent squad leader even if he was a wise guy, nor the staff sergeant, who the young buck sergeant thought was okay, even if he was a bit of a prick. The 19-year-old "shake-and-bake" sergeant might have been a 90-day wonder, but he knew his shit. Any serious misgivings the staff sergeant had about the Wise Guy gave way before the red-white-and-black 75th Ranger scroll the young buck sergeant wore above his Cav patch. The Wise Guy had been a LRRP with Hotel Company, and he had earned a Silver Star for gallantry. He was a smart-ass but a competent soldier, which infuriated the professional soldier to no end. The peg didn't quite fit, and the young yahoo wasn't helping matters any.

Once, after he had been shot through both thighs while walking point, AK-47 bullets ripping apart his left hamstring and right abductor muscle, the Wise Guy hadn't been so cocky. The bullets that also had fractured his right hip took away something more than blood and flesh. But the kid bounced back and returned to the platoon, and in doing so, he had earned the staff sergeant's respect. On the other hand, the Wise Guy's jokes had kept the wise-guy buck sergeant from crossing over to being what Burrows considered a real soldier.

On the other hand, the Wise Guy sometimes thought of Burrows as a humorless zealot who liked the Army and the whole nine yards of its bullshit. What was worse, perhaps unforgivable, was that Burrows hated rock and roll! The guy thought Crosby, Stills, and Nash were three new replacements in the third squad! The trouble was, the Wise Guy reluctantly respected the professional soldier because, well, the guy knew his shit. Maybe he didn't quite get all of the Wise Guy's punch lines or really understand when he was joking, and maybe he played his classical music too damn loud, but he was a good soldier. The asshole.

In one firefight in the Dog's Head region of Tay Ninh, the Wise Guy once saw Burrows assault an enemy fighting position, using semiautomatic fire to keep the NVA soldier who occupied it too busy to take a careful aim. Burrows' advance gave a few soldiers in the second squad time to find protective cover. He probably saved their lives by killing the enemy soldier before turning his attention back to help the point squad who had their hands busy in close, sometimes hand-to-hand jungle battle.

The Blues had been inserted in a 25th Infantry Division area of operations along the Cambodian border to check out what they were told was a deserted bunker complex, only it wasn't. The 21-man reconnaissance platoon managed to run into a reinforced company from the 95C NVA Division. Outnumbered four to one, the Blues could only fight it out. When the fighting had finally subsided, 39 NVA soldiers were dead and in sight, while four of the Blues had been wounded—all in the point squad, which had borne the brunt of the enemy's ground assault.

During that one firefight, the Wise Guy earned Burrows' respect, and the Wise Guy came to view the professional soldier in a different light. Of course, that didn't mean they wouldn't argue—or periodically agree, as they were now doing in the Blues' command post. The Wise Guy, sitting across from Burrows in the rescue force's assembly area, nodded along with the acting platoon seargant's comment about waiting it out and going in when the weather cleared. That was something they did see eye to eye on. It didn't take an optometrist to see they were the LRRPs' last real hope. As with the rest of the troop, the Blues Platoon was an eclectic mix of people and notions: whites mostly, with a small number of blacks, Hispanics, a Canadian or two, and the occasional Asian-American. They were draftees; enlistees; pro war; antiwar; city boys, street smart and caustic; slow-talking country types whose speech patterns at times belied their intelligence. There was also an occasional intruder from the suburbs of America, who thought that the faces on Mount Rushmore were a natural phenomenon. Some were better soldiers than others, but most were a cut above others of their rank or skill. Over the course of their tours, they'd learn to rely on each other in ways most people would never imagine—or for those who could, in ways they prayed to God they wouldn't have to.

Through sudden jungle firefights, ambushes, sniper attacks, ground probes, and combat assaults, they learned to depend upon each other, and in some ways, they'd become family. Most had never really had any close dealings with people outside their own neighborhoods back home, let alone their own ethnic backgrounds, so the war provided them with lessons in sociology no school could ever offer.

Friendships were slow to form and appeared in clusters, in small pockets that spanned cultural and ethnic differences. From those friendships, bonds were created and unspoken alliances were made. Friends weren't just "friends"—they were "buddies," the Army's catchall term for the guys who looked out for one another. A buddy was trusted to do the job he was trained to do—and more. He covered your ass in a firefight or pulled you behind cover when you were wounded. Each combat action amplified and defined the friendship, and friends of friends became friends. Their causes became sympathetic.

And no cause took on more value or importance than helping a buddy in combat. It was a lesson learned in the shaking fear and aftermath of a small, tense firefight; of a helicopter crash; of a rocket or mortar attack; of watching friends die doing their best to keep you from dying; of knowing that, maybe, just once, you could rely on someone to be there for you or to try everything he could to get there to help—not for politics, not because someone said so, but because it mattered. Because you were a buddy, even if you were a hard-nosed professional soldier determined to win the war sometime during his tour, or a wise-guy buck sergeant who was only interested in seeing that his people got home safely.

One year earlier, Lieutenant R. B. Alexander of San Clemente, California, was accompanying the Blues on a routine mission out in the jungles in the province. The Blues Platoon leader at that time was a regular line officer pilot who had been handed the job but who didn't feel he was up to the task of leading the recon platoon. He asked Alexander to come along on the patrol in the hopes of having him take over the job. It wasn't that the pilot was incompetent, it was just that the young warrant officer felt he could do a better job of fighting the war from a helicopter.

On the insertion, the lead helicopter took fire and crashed, and the second aircraft in line fell victim as well. Six members of the recon platoon were instantly dead, and others were seriously injured. As the enemy began to quickly retreat from the trap he'd set, Alexander went into action, setting up a perimeter while yelling for the radioman to call for a medevac for the wounded. "You!" he yelled to a young NCO who was having his machine gunner lay down a base of supporting fire. "What's your name?"

"Smart, sir."

"Sergeant Smart, get some people to cover the other side of the landing zone."

"Yes sir!" he said, carrying out the order while Alexander tried to figure out just what to do next. The Blues

Platoon leader let Alexander take the helm because he could see Alexander knew what to do. What was more, he saw that the men were responding to the commands. Meanwhile, he worked on trying to help the medic with the wounded. Later, when there was time to think about what happened, the platoon leader talked his decision over with the troop commander, who was satisfied with the decision, provided Lieutenant Alexander agreed.

"You take the platoon. I'm going back to flying," the Blues Platoon leader said later, while Alexander tried to talk him out of his decision.

Lieutenant Alexander reminded the platoon leader that what had happened at the LZ wasn't his fault. "It's your platoon," he said. "They need you."

The platoon leader shook his head. "No. After today they'll need to rebuild, and then they'll need someone who knows what he's doing. I'm a pilot. I was out of my element out there today. The platoon's yours if you want the job. I'm going back to where I can do some good. So what do you say?"

Lieutenant Alexander nodded and offered his hand. "Thanks," he said. The pilot shook his hand. With little more fanfare or words the pilot turned his platoon over to Alexander. Sergeant Smart was one hell of a squad leader—as were Sergeants Gill, Gibson, and Espino—and Doc Adams, the platoon medic, was nothing short of amazing, so taking over the platoon was something Alexander was pleased to do. Over the next few months under his leadership, the Blues became a tight, effective reconnaissance platoon and rescue force. Robert Gill had been a former LRRP; his jungle fighting skills were impressive.

And what he didn't know, the platoon helped teach him. Specialist Ron Aiman, the platoon's primary radioman, was Alexander's right hand. The new platoon leader was convinced that Aiman always knew what was going down, sometimes even before Alexander or the others caught on.

Blues men were all remarkable, and firefight after firefight, rescue after rescue, their deeds proved it to Alexander. They were his Blues, his people, and he was proud to lead them. Over time and with arrivals and departures, the troop and the platoon changed personnel, but the makeup and attitude was basically the same. The men of the troop knew the Blues were special just because of the job they did. And even if they didn't really believe it, those who led them knew otherwise.

Alexander had known it, the new platoon leader who followed him knew it, and Lieutenant Jack Hugele knew it too when he called for volunteers for the Ranger rescue mission. "We wait," Lieutenant Hugele said in the platoon command post as some volunteers shifted their positions while trying to catch some much needed rest. Others, like Burrows and the Wise Guy, checked and rechecked their weapons and equipment—sometimes out of anxiety and sometimes out of professionalism.

"So tell me again about the Roman grunts?" the Wise Guy asked while Burrows waited to see if he was just being a smart-ass. When he finally decided the young buck sergeant was asking seriously, he gave his answer.

"Like what?"

"A while back you said something about how they carried more than today's grunts do."

The staff sergeant nodded. "Uh-huh. They carried everything with them, from surveying equipment to their full arm of weapons . . ."

"Like what? I mean you always see them in the movies with a sword and a spear," the Wise Guy said as he was tearing down his M16.

"Two throwing spears actually, at least toward the late

days of the Republic. One had a head of tempered iron and the other was left in its untempered state . . ."

"Why?" the wise-guy sergeant asked.

"So the one end would cut into the enemy's shield while bending the other point . . ."

"Why?"

Burrows, slightly annoyed at the interruption, continued his story anyway, "So it would make the enemy's shield useless, and before you ask about the spear," he added quickly, "if one end was bent, then it wouldn't be very effective if the enemy threw it back at you."

Thinking that over for a few seconds, the Wise Guy nodded. "Makes sense," he said. "But what about everything they carried? What did it weigh?"

"About 60 pounds on average. Enough food for three days, a mess kit, a pickax, a chain, hook, a saw, stakes, and a wicker basket for moving earth for their entrenchments. Wanna know something else, hotshot?" The Wise Guy nodded. Burrows was better than an encyclopedia. "In 1920, some archaeologists found Roman artifacts here in Vietnam."

"Get the fuck out of here!"

"No, seriously. In fact, they're in a museum near Saigon. It was destiny that brought them here, too!" he said quietly.

"You really like this shit, don't you?" The Wise Guy stopped what he was doing and stared at Burrows.

"The war?"

The wise-guy sergeant nodded.

"Man has been fighting throughout recorded history," Burrows explained. "That's a given, and quite probably long before that, judging from everything anthropologists tell us. Thousands of years later, we're still fighting. The only difference between us and the cavemen is that when they saw their enemy, they began clubbing him right away. Modern man likes to talk for five minutes before the clubbing starts. All I know is that every civilization or society relies on its soldiers. Some praise them more than others, but sooner or later, they all rely on them. It's a necessary profession, and it always has been and always will be."

The younger sergeant smiled and shook his head. It was time to play "fuck with the lifer" again. "So, like, is Burrows a classical Italian name or did they call you Burrowelli?"

Burrows just shook his head. Every so often, the Wise Guy could really make him laugh. But not this time. "Fuck you," he said.

"That doesn't sound Italian either," the Wise Guy said. "You got any cleaning oil?" he asked while blowing dust out of the rifle's bolt and wiping the already clean metal with a dry cloth.

"Would you settle for olive oil?" Burrows asked, handing the point man a small squeeze bottle.

"Who do I look like? Popeye?"

Burrows laughed. "Dennis the Menace maybe and maybe a halfway decent point man, too, for such a smart-ass."

"Halfway, huh?"

The Wise Guy looked hurt, but Burrows knew better. "Yeah, and that's only because of your nose."

"My what?"

"Your nose," the staff sergeant explained. "I read somewhere that between the eyes there's the ethmoid bone, which in some people is sensitive to the earth's magnetic core. Supposedly it helps the sense of direction."

"This is bullshit, right?"

"No, it's true. To tell you the truth, I also think you're better than the tracker dogs."

Obviously proud of himself, the Wise Guy beamed. "Really?"

"Uh-huh. But only because you don't shit on the trail.

You ever think about making the Army a career?" Staff Sergeant Burrows asked straight-faced and serious, which caught the buck sergeant by surprise.

"No," he said thoughtfully. "Not really."

The staff sergeant smiled. "Good," he said; the kid still had a way to go.

# CHAPTER THIRTEEN

Before Royce Clark was carried from the kill zone, he had managed to grab part of the team's aid bag. But they had just one syringe of morphine between them, and Andrus gave it to Clark. The team medic was twisting in pain, writhing and rocking from side to side because of the pain from his splintered leg. His face was flushed, and the infection that had set in because of the dirt, debris, and humidity left him bathed in sweat. He was lapsing in and out of consciousness.

The injection of morphine would only provide him with a temporary escape. Maybe eight hours, at best. If they had eight hours. Then the pain would return tenfold. How Clark would handle that was something he'd think about when the time came.

Andrus' own sense of dread spread with his pain. While he and Clark might've wondered from time to time what being wounded was like and how they would handle the situation, they had also known that until it happened they could never understand. Now any speculation and guessing was gone. It was real, and nothing like either had imagined. Surviving was everything. They'd endure the pain and try to hold out.

To the 20-year-old Ranger radioman who was weakened by his own wounds and blood loss, the decision to give the morphine to Clark had been the right thing to do. Clark needed it more. Andrus was still holding on, in spite of the pressure building in his chest and his damaged wrist and shoulder.

He felt around his back and stomach area and confirmed his suspicions. He could feel no exit wound, so he knew the bullet was lodged somewhere in his chest. The wound burned, and at times, he sensed his own temperature rising uncomfortably. The weather was a cold downpour, but his forehead and chest were hot at the same time that his hands and feet were wet and cold.

Mostly, though, he was dizzy. Ron Andrus found himself fighting to keep everything from spinning to a disoriented end. Sleep was out of the question, and he feared that if he passed out, he might never wake up, so lying on the wet, orange ground and fighting to keep from closing his eyes, the Ranger radioman studied the black velvet jungle with growing fear and anticipation.

Gripping his M16, Ron Andrus' thought went from the ambush site to his present position, running the events over and over again but deriving little comfort from the replay of events when he did.

Whenever he tried to figure out exactly what had happened, he got stuck on one painful aspect—the team leader and assistant team leader they'd left behind. If only he could've grabbed Cochrane and pulled him back, he thought, but there was no solace in the wishful thinking. Jesus! Was Cochrane still alive, or had he died from the bullet wound? In all likelihood, both bodies had been riddled with bullets when the NVA overran their positions, but that conclusion didn't provide Andrus with solace.

Realistically, there wasn't anything he could have done. But while he was alive and hiding in the underbrush, the thought of leaving his buddies' bodies behind plagued him.

Never mind that the enemy had four of the five-man team in the ambush kill zone, or that the amount of rifle and machine-gun fire the enemy had thrown at them had left the area a fragmented mess. Never mind, too, that he and Clark had both been seriously wounded and that the team leader had saved their lives by ordering them back, choosing to cover their escape as they moved, only to take a bullet or burst in the throat.

Ron Andrus felt he should have done more; a common LRRP/Ranger dilemma.

Time and again it was drilled into the Rangers that they were the best. And with the remarkable success the company had enjoyed, it was no wonder many of the young Rangers believed that they were in some ways super-soldiers. Invincible by practice and success.

In many ways, they *were* the best at what they did. But they weren't invincible, and their human frailties were sometimes brought to their attention in ways that were less than subtle. The small size of their teams enabled them to move and maneuver more quickly and quietly than their enemy. But the team's small size worked against the Rangers once contact was made. On a five-man team, one casualty reduced a team's effectiveness by 20 percent. It didn't take much sophisticated math for Andrus to conclude that their team was down almost 80 percent, and the fifth player was struggling to stay in the game and dramatically change the odds.

Clark wasn't moaning as loudly. The morphine appeared to be working. Andrus watched over Clark while keeping a vigil on the surrounding countryside. Not that he could see much anyway, let alone keep the NVA back if they blundered into the position. He knew the enemy was out there scouring the rain forest for the Rangers. Time and again, he thought he heard branches breaking nearby. But it might have been just the rain or his imagination.

Suddenly, the loud report of a rifle shot settled the question, and Andrus, back on edge, got his adrenaline pumping again. The NVA were coming, and the war, his war, was about to get closer.

Ron Andrus didn't believe he was better in the bush than any other LRRP in the company, but he was part of the company, and in his three months with it, he had seen the teams pull off amazing patrols. Success had become so much a habit to the LRRPs that many of them nourished the illusion that it would always remain with them. The wonder of it all is that, given the nature of the patrols, more teams weren't hit as hard as Andrus' had been. Or worse.

Patrolling in small teams in enemy territory was a numbers game, and eventually a price was paid.

Another single gunshot rang through the foggy, moonless night. Andrus studied the wall of vegetation before him as he heard the rustle of the underbrush. The enemy was moving closer, but the weather had covered the survivors' escape. The NVA couldn't pick up a trail.

They were, however, working a circular pattern, checking as much of the immediate countryside as they could in the dark.

A grenade would do it, he thought. Just one grenade tossed out between them, and the NVA wouldn't know what hit them or where it came from. Of course, if any survived, they would know about how close the LRRPs were. But neither he nor Clark had any grenades left. Everything had been used in the kill zone or dropped as the LRRPs retreated. They were lucky to have escaped with their weapons.

Because the bullets and shrapnel had cut into the trees and underbrush, the smell of gunpowder had given way to the pungent odor of freshly cut vegetation. It smelled as if someone had mowed the lawn there.

Squeezing the black plastic stock of the M16 and remaining quiet, the Ranger radioman waited for his target to appear. The tension and blood loss left him weak, but he wasn't about to give in to debility. He had to hold on. He'd fight them on his terms. On Ranger terms, which meant you used every means to your advantage.

There could be no surrender because the NVA didn't take LRRPs prisoner, not with the bounty on them. And there was the matter of their wounds; the enemy wouldn't waste medicine, which was difficult for him to get, on Americans.

Even if they were somehow captured alive and survived without proper medical attention, then what? Live in some jungle prison in a small bamboo cage to rot away? Not likely. Few prisoners survived captivity in the jungle because if the war or the enemy didn't kill them right off, then malaria, a rat or snakebite, or any one of a hundred different ailments would waste them away in months.

It was usually downed pilots and ranking officers who were sent north to the real prisons; the rest were left to wither and die in the jungles as slaves or sideshows.

As the rustling of the underbrush diminished, the signal shots rang out again, this time in the distance, fading into the night. It was apparent, even to Andrus in his weakened state, that, unable to track the surviving Americans in the poor weather, the North Vietnamese Army soldiers were moving on. The jungle and the rain forests that so often had hidden the NVA soldiers' safe havens and firing positions were now working for the wounded Rangers.

Darkness was one of the few breaks Andrus or Clark would get that day. But morning would come, and when it did, the NVA would be able to search for sign of their prey.

And the weather was bound to clear up eventually.

What then?

# CHAPTER FOURTEEN

Phuoc Binh province was also known as Song Be after the dun-colored river that lazily snaked its way through the plush green hills and valleys and finally out of the southernmost reaches of Military Region II or II Corps of South Vietnam.

From the foot of the Central Highlands, it flowed down into Military Region III, III Corps, twisting and coiling past the rolling tropical jungle outside of Apache Troop's new home at Fire Support Base Buttons. A surprisingly strong current moved beneath the orange silt-covered surface, and at night, the heavy lingering muck and musk smell of the ancient rain forest crept up and over its banks like some primordial creature too powerful to stop.

The troop had been reassigned to Buttons to help put a crimp in the Viet Cong's and NVA's increased activity in the region. Caught in transition, part of the unit was still at Tay Ninh West, while the rest were either at the fire support base or temporarily housed at Phuoc Vinh. Because it was primarily an exit point for one of the major infiltration routes of the Ho Chi Minh Trail, the town of Song Be and the Army's fire support base adjacent to it were frequent targets of enemy attacks, whether it was the almost daily mortar or rocket attacks or large-scale ground attacks.

In November of the previous year, the North Vietnamese Army ventured a large-scale ground assault on the small outpost. In their typical predawn assault pattern, the NVA companies moved within striking distance from the American base, got up on line, and after a bugle's cry, the hundreds of soldiers charged the barbed-wire perimeter. Pushed back and repelled again and again by the defenders in a costly battle, the North Vietnamese stoically retreated to lick their wounds. Then, later in the year, they tried again, always probing and pushing to get inside and overrun Buttons after a sinister barrage of rocket and mortar fire.

Destroyed in the 1968 Tet offensive, Song Be was struggling to come back with moderate success. In the two years that followed, the enemy had not achieved his one New Year's success. However, it didn't keep him from trying. If the defenders on Buttons had learned anything about their enemy, it was that he was patient and determined.

Nicknamed Rocket Alley, the town and fire support base took a heavy pounding from the enemy every time the opportunity presented itself. The last major assault on Fire Support Base Buttons had left scores of enemies wounded and dead in the strands of barbed wire that encircled the base.

The Americans had paid as well when the communists' ground-attack forces pushed through the barbed wire and between several of the perimeter bunkers before being driven out with a fierce counterattack by the Cobra attack helicopters, leveled artillery pieces, and survival instincts and determination of those who occupied the base. The North Vietnamese were learning something of the determination of their enemy as well.

While many believed there were no front lines in the war, those who occupied the fire support base knew otherwise. There was no doubt in anyone's mind that this was a front line, just as there was no doubt who owned the jungle countryside outside of the barbed-wire perimeter. But owning it and making use of it were two different things, and the helicopter-borne units such as Apache Troop, the grunts who operated out of the outpost, along with the 105mm and 155mm howitzers from the artillery battery that was stationed there as well, made owning the region a costly proposition for the North Vietnamese Army divisions and Viet Cong battalions.

Somewhere in the region, just beyond the perimeter, the sounds of the no-name battles could always be heard: small-arm or machine-gun fire, explosions from grenades, artillery rounds, rockets, mortars, or the mute ripping sound of the attack helicopter's miniguns tearing into the jungle.

At night they became more apparent and were accented by the red and green tracer rounds darting around them from the U.S. and communist forces exchanging fire. The brief, pale-white glow of falling star clusters or parachute flares against the seemingly black velvet jungle and the ghostlike green sheen from the larger artillery illumination rounds added to the show.

During the working day and long into the evening, there was always the chopping sound of the helicopter rotor blades. In the early-morning hours just beyond midnight, though, the pancake-shaped base would become oddly quiet, and the sounds in the near hills would take over, reminding everyone who lived on Buttons that the war was still on and that safety was just the illusion of distance. Joe Sparacino, Apache Troop's first sergeant, was determined to give the illusion some basis in fact.

Constantly inspecting the troop's new perimeter line and accompanying bunker fighting positions, Sparacino, with Staff Sergeant Burrows in tow, would make recommendations and suggestions. While the perimeter line had yet to be completed, any holes in the defense were quickly filled by Sparacino's critical eye. Claymore antipersonnel mines were set, Willie Pete—white phosphorous—grenades were fashioned into booby traps, and myriad trip flares were added to protect the perimeter line.

When he and Burrows were satisfied with their assessment the Italian-American turned his attention toward providing better living conditions for his men. In this mudhole, that was the major battle.

As the volunteers from Apache Troop waited for the weather to clear, the early morning was unusually punctuated with the sound of readying helicopters.

After McIntosh's and Fuller's return, the crews worked to ensure that everything, including the radios, would be ready for the mission, whenever it came.

An hour before sunrise, or before it normally would rise had it not been for the poor weather, the volunteers were stirring again. First light meant the mission was on, at least to the point of getting airborne and heading toward Cambodia. However, the fog was reluctant to cooperate with the ceiling, now back up to a little over 50 feet. The hope was that at some point between Fire Support Base Buttons and Fire Support Base David the weather would break.

The Air Force's weather specialists had predicted clear skies after the fog burned off, but just how long that would take was subject to anyone's guess. In the flatland regions, it was safe to assume that by midday the sun would be able to clear away even the most obstinate fog. The rolling hills of Song Be and similar countryside of neighboring Cambodia were another matter entirely. While the sun could burn away the stubborn fog at the hilltops at higher levels, the small valleys and depressions would cling to their pools of fog well into the afternoon. The Cambodian countryside looked like islands of plush green vegetation surrounded in an ocean of gray fog. It would lift. Eventually.

But that was later. For the immediate now, in the hour that preceded daylight, the volunteers were shifting about, bored from the hours of waiting and uncertainty, while the pilots and officers were in the Song Be TOC discussing the status of the mission. Some were in favor of a quick departure, while others were less than enthusiastic.

"It's too dangerous," one pilot said, while McIntosh, his eyes red and tired from a restless night, smirked.

"Yeah, to wait," he said. The sarcasm loaded and pointed at the critic who should have known better than to go one-on-one with McIntosh. The feisty Seattle native had a reputation for speaking his mind. "Are you willing to write them off?"

The second pilot didn't answer. It wasn't as much a shame tactic as it was a gut-wrenching question. A majority of the pilots of Apache Troop had been shot down at one time or another, and they knew what it was like to be on the ground in enemy-held territory, hoping to God that someone, anyone, was on the way to rescue them.

While the pilots had the Blue Platoon, knowing the 17 to 25 infantry soldiers would scramble to rescue them on such occasions, they also could rely on the nearest LRRP/Ranger team for backup if they were in the area. To say a bond existed between the LRRPs of Hotel Company and the 1st of the 9th was putting it mildly. Everybody knew it, and everybody at one time or another had inserted or extracted a Ranger team. Some had even earned medals of gallantry for saving the lives of the wounded LRRPs. Like Captain Kit Beatton who, while extracting a team that had been hit by a larger enemy unit in a running gun battle, had learned that one of the five-man patrol was severely wounded and lying back on a jungle trail. The four LRRPs who were all wounded and struggling to board Beatton's helicopter excitedly pointed back into the jungle. Meanwhile, the North Vietnamese Army unit in pursuit was firing on the helicopter, while Apache Troop gunships did their best to keep the enemy at bay.

"One . . . one of my people . . ." the Ranger team leader

yelled to the officer over the noise of the battle and the constant whopping of the helicopter's blades.

All of the LRRPs were bleeding and in no shape to go back for the fifth man, and Beatton knew that his crew chief and door gunner were keeping the enemy back with their machine-gun fire.

"Take it!" he yelled to his copilot while he hurriedly undid his safety harness and climbed out of the Huey. Armed with only a .38, Beatton disappeared into the tree line and then, a lifetime later, returned with the wounded Ranger over his shoulder.

"Let's get out of here!" he yelled to the crew chief, laying the wounded LRRP on the cargo bay floor and climbing in after him.

Beatton, a short time later, would be awarded a Silver Star for gallantry at the recommendation of a grateful Ranger company.

The three troops of the squadron were their immediate backup support and sometimes their only real shot at survival. The small Ranger patrols were always outnumbered and always behind the enemy lines, so when they were found out, the situations always became close and tense.

"We don't leave our people," McIntosh said at Song Be. "We ain't going to write them off."

"At ease!" a ranking officer said, quelling the argument. McIntosh was right, and everyone knew it. Now all that remained was the strategy.

"If we can get above it, then we'll be halfway to David when the sun burns it off." There was no doubt that the Seattle native was going up again. It was now just a matter of who'd be going up with him.

"And if it doesn't burn off?" asked the critic.

"Then we try it on instruments again," said McIntosh.

"Let's send up a test ship," the critic countered. "At least that way we'll know."

"Fine! I'll go up again."

"No, you won't," said another pilot, Warrant Officer John C. Bartlett, one of Apache Troop's gunship jockeys. "It's my turn." Sticking his head outside and taking in the fog cover, Bartlett said, "Fuck it!" to himself, went back in the TOC, and picked up his flight helmet. "I'm going to David. I need an X ray," the Whitefish, Montana, resident said, surveying the room.

He found his gunner in Warrant Officer Tyrone Graham, who grinned and said, "That's me, partner. Let's go." The argument was settled; the pilots headed out of the briefing area and sauntered toward the flight line, while in Tay Ninh, Blue, Lieutenant Hugele, rounded up his platoon. Chief Warrant Officer Glen R. Senkowski was in the TOC in Tay Ninh as a hasty plan was being formulated there. Monitoring the Ranger team's progress was also a responsibility of Apache Troop, and Senkowski would have been the pilot to extract the team had everything gone according to plan. On strip alert as the ready pilot, Senkowski sensed something was wrong early on when the Ranger relay station at Fire Support Base David couldn't raise the missing patrol. He felt his stomach begin to twist and turn knowing that after an hour of trying, the relay couldn't reach the team. Something was wrong and he knew it, and standing by monitoring the radio traffic, he had a sick feeling also, knowing he wouldn't be needed to extract the team. All through the night, he waited by the radios for the connection that never came. The rescue force would have their hands full going after them, and with all of the pilots they needed for the rescue mission; Senkowski remained in the TOC, listening as the small audience grew. After all, the drama was still being played out.

The Blues rescue force was ready on the predawn flight line dividing up into the teams for the three Huey lift ships that were cranking up behind their L-shaped, sandbagged revetments. At the controls of the lead ship, Warrant Officer Bill McIntosh waited for the thumbs-up sign from Art Dockter, his crew chief for the mission. Once cranked and readied, the awkward-looking aircraft hovered out of its safe place and lumbered over to the flight line. Touching down, the Blues quickly loaded into its open belly, and within minutes, the Huey lift ship lifted a few feet off of the ground, dipped its bulbed nose, and roared down the flight line following the lead of Bartlett's Cobra gunship. Those two aircraft were followed by the second two lift ships, each allowing a buffer of a few minutes of distance and airspeed to compensate for the bad weather. Nobody spoke on the wet and bumpy ride out. The rescue mission was on and their focus was on what lay ahead.

# CHAPTER FIFTEEN

At 2100 hours, the Cambodian evening was unusually quiet, and when the rain finally did ease, the night lingered in fog. The fog was thinning but holding, and while the hours advanced, Hancock knew it was as good as it was going to get. Cold, stiff, and aching, he got to his feet, knowing he couldn't wait. There wasn't time. As he started forward across the open dead-man's land that separated the jungle's edge from the outpost, he knew what he had to do.

A hundred yards or so to make it to the perimeter wire. An easy walk by most standards unless you're being hunted or unless you're moving toward a base where a nervous soldier could easily mistake you for the enemy.

Since he knew the grunts would have their two-man listening posts out as an early warning for any large force moving toward David, he knew he had to carefully skirt those positions. Any sudden movement or noise on his part, and the grunts might just shoot first and regret it later, so Hancock crawled around the position working toward the fire support base.

Once he made it within 20 or so yards, he grabbed the white silk of a spent parachute flare and slowly rose to his feet.

"Don't shoot!" he yelled, uncertain whether the perimeter guards on David had heard him or not. Was he shouting?

"Don't shoot! I'm a Ranger! Please don't shoot! I'm coming in!"

Over his head he began waving the small white parachute from the extinguished flare. Hopefully, the universal sign of surrender would keep the tired and startled grunts on the hastily completed, rough-textured fire support base from opening fire.

Ironically, the hundred yards of open space he had crossed and was now firmly established in was referred to as dead-man's land. Each of the forward support bases was designed with the open space to buffer any surprise or sneak attacks. Closer to the small jungle outpost, just a few yards beyond the perimeter bunker or fighting line, were three distinct lines of waist-high barbed wire serving as the real barrier between the jungle and the small camp. In between the barbed wire the division engineers responsible for creating these small outposts had thrown in a row of tanglefoot—the ankle-high barbed-wire fence that was designed to trip up anyone who had made it through one of the three barbed-wire barriers. The 8th Engineers were usually given anywhere from two days' to one week's advance notice of a base's opening. Then, the first contingent of Army construction personnel would be lifted in shortly after the grunts secured the proposed site. Operating in teams, the engineers would go to work. With working plans in place, they'd clear away any natural obstacles with explosives or chain saws before bringing in the heavy equipment that would complete the job.

Case 450 garden spreaders, D-5 bulldozers, and backhoes were ferried in to level the proposed sites. Berms, the ringed walls of dirt, were pushed into place to form a perimeter as well as the fixed artillery placements for the base's big guns while the spreaders cleared areas for the barbed wire. Backhoes went about the task of creating bunkers for guard or command-post positions, and during it all, the engineers took the same enemy sniper, mortar, or rocket fire the grunts did as they hurried about their work.

The fire support bases had to set up by dark of day one. Any finishing touches were left to the grunts if there was time, which usually there wasn't. The North Vietnamese Army and Viet Cong knew the longer they gave these outposts the more difficult it would be to overrun them, so within the opening hours of the proposed sites, the enemy went about his job of making the bases a costly project.

Most fire support bases in Vietnam had the luxury of time, while in Cambodia the situation pushed up the parameters of the clock. Outposts like David were short-term and short-lived, so the emphasis on attacking them was intensified. After the engineers left, the grunts had to add their own special touches, but not out of comfort as much as out of necessity.

Between the barbed-wire and tanglefoot barriers, the base defenders planted their claymore antipersonnel mines, along with trip wires for the trip flares that would offer advance warning if any part of someone's body managed to snag the small, thin metal line it was rigged to.

The new concertina wire with its razor-sharp edges was beginning to replace the slinky tube-like rolls of barbed wire, while some bases relied on combinations of the old and the new to act as a deterrent.

David was a hastily erected forward fire support base. In fact, it was the furthermost fire support base in Cambodia, and smack in the center of the Ho Chi Minh Trail.

FSB David was a fortified laager for D Company, the 1st of the 5th Cav, who knew their makeshift base was short-term and temporary. Its whole purpose was to serve as a thorn in the NVA's side in a blocking posture against the retreating enemy units. After all, elements of the 1st Cav Division had the task of coming in behind the North Vietnamese Army and Viet Cong forces and attacking them as they withdrew.

The outpost wouldn't be on anybody's map for too long. It was not intended to be. Its defenses were incomplete, and the soldiers that occupied it relied on the few rows of concertina wire and the small berm and ring of fighting positions that guarded the artillery pieces it employed.

Continuous ground attacks gave the small outpost a siege mentality. Too many times, the enemy would hit it with heavy rockets and mortars, followed by his commando sapper raids or large-scale ground assaults. David had been hit only a few days before and almost overrun, but the grunts held on and drove them back with courage and tenacity.

The odd thing was that Fire Support Base David was only a temporary facility; one the Army didn't plan on having any permanence. It was there to assist the push into Cambodia and to be abandoned when they pulled out. Nothing would be left to the enemy but the open knoll it occupied. Even then, the grunts would booby-trap it, leaving little surprises for the enemy to stumble across when he eventually combed through the site.

As Hancock moved, the grunts fired a succession of flares, taking immediate notice of the lone figure walking toward their perimeter. Within seconds, the evening was filled with the sounds of rifle bolts slamming forward as weary eyes squinted over rifle sights and frenzied fingers flipped the rifle selector switches from safe to automatic fire, the spring-loaded metallic clicks as distinct as the NVA's single rifle shots hours before. Within minutes, yelling could be heard across the small base.

Hancock had gotten their attention, as the rifle barrels aimed in on the thin mud-covered soldier whose nationality or purpose could be anybody's guess.

"Don't shoot!" he said again. "I'm American. I'm a Ranger! We were ambushed. I'm coming in!"

In basic and advanced infantry training soldiers are taught to bring the individual to a stop by calling, "Halt! Who goes there?" followed by a second command of, "Advance to be recognized."

When the approaching individual is close enough to speak within a normal tone of voice, the soldier on guard might then ask for the password before allowing the person to proceed.

In combat, there is often little time for such formalities, and an individual's life or death might largely depend upon what the soldier on guard thinks he sees and what he can instantly assess.

In Hancock's case, the grunts were briefed and knew what to expect, so when they called him forward and rushed out to meet him, it was to bring him to safety as quickly as possible. Hancock's uniform was filthy and displaying the holes from sharp branches and thorns. His hands revealed small cuts and thin amber lines were evident on his face. He was tired to the point of exhaustion, and armed with only a knife, he had somehow made it back.

For the Ranger radio-relay station and the Ranger company, their worst fears were confirmed. The LRRP team had been hit, and so far they only had one survivor; one survivor whose cut, dazed, and ragged appearance left many of the grunts on David wondering just what in the hell had happened, while maybe secretly and not so secretly thanking God it hadn't happened to them.

". . . Ambush," he said, turning back toward the jungle, only no one really needed to hear it to understand.

"Where are the others?" someone asked. With everyone crowding around, it was difficult seeing who was asking the question. More than likely it was the Ranger's radio-relay man on the base who was pushing his way to Hancock.

"Andrus and Clark . . . still out there," said the Ranger weakly. "They're wounded . . . hiding. We got to get them."

"We will," Spaulding, the Ranger's radio-relay man, replied, taking Hancock by the arm. "Don't worry. We'll find them."

Specialist Don Spaulding had his own reasons for wanting to find the others. Originally scheduled to go out on the mission with Team 5-2, a doctor's orders pulled him at the last minute. These were his teammates, too, and the loss would gnaw away at him more than it first appeared.

"We'll find them," he said again, knowing he'd have to pass on the grim news to Phuoc Vinh. It wasn't the kind of news anyone wanted to share.

Any psychological edge the grunts enjoyed before Hancock's arrival was lost in the realization of what had happened. To many, the Airborne Ranger epitomized everything a real soldier should be. Throughout basic and advanced training, as well as anything that involved marching or running, each and every soldier in the Army, from the lowest private to the commanding general, had sung the praises of the Airborne Rangers.

Across every U.S. Army base or installation in the forts or camps around the world, the soldiers sang the familiar cadences:

> I want to be an Airborne Ranger,
> I want to live a life of danger.
> I want to go to Vietnam.
> I want to kill a Viet Cong.
> Airborne! Ranger!
> Up the hill! Down the hill! Around the hill!
> Airborne! Ranger!

Even if the soldiers didn't really believe the Rangers were the best of the best, they knew they couldn't be that far behind. They were snake-eaters. They could live off of the land and navigate any terrain! They could make weapons of anything they could find, and use them, too!

They could get the job done. Any job. They were all volunteers! All gung ho and Jesus! Even in Vietnam, they would run for miles in the staggering heat as part of their training!

Everyone knew they were good, even if they sometimes didn't like to admit it.

Staring at the Ranger in their midst, this surviving LRRP, the grunts began to wonder what the team had run into. Catching bits and pieces of his story as they moved back into the fire support base, a few grunts turned back to the dark, threatening, rolling countryside, knowing that the NVA that ambushed and chased the survivor were still out there. Waiting.

The listening posts were reporting movement before Hancock showed up, and in the short period of time they occupied the small outpost, the grunts of D Company knew it was still the enemy's area of operations, still his home turf. Every American soldier knew the momentum was on their side—for as long as it rolled! The trouble was with the imposed limits of the raid, the politically imposed 20-plus miles they were allowed to advance, which kept them from rolling over the retreating NVA and Viet Cong! Like a watchdog on a leash, they could only run so far before the chain began to choke back. The NVA and Viet Cong knew the political furor the raid had caused in the United States and that President Nixon couldn't advance any further. Like the interloper who figured out the length of the watchdog's chain, the NVA and Viet Cong were keeping their distance while working on a plan to get beyond the watchdog and do a little snarling of their own. Eventually the Americans would have to withdraw, and when they did, the enemy would begin closing in around them.

The raid or incursion was in its waning days, but the fighting was far from over as evidenced by Hancock's lone escape. The Americans would retreat sooner or later, and when they did, the NVA and Viet Cong would carry out one of the principles they learned over the ages: attacking the enemy as he retreated. Besides, there were only so many avenues of approach and escape. That's where the NVA and VC would hit, while how to attack the Air Cav units became another problem entirely.

Their success with the chance encounter of the American Ranger unit gave them new hopes. The "men with the painted faces," as the enemy referred to the Rangers because of the green-black-and-sand-colored camouflage paint they wore, were the 1st Cav's ghost soldiers, and if they could catch them, then they could catch anyone, which was something even the grunts on David were thinking.

The frustration and anguish that was on the Ranger's face was shared by them all.

"Jesus! I thought we were winning this thing!" a young grunt said, studying the Ranger who was being led to safety.

"We were, kid," a vet said behind him. "Until the politicians announced to the world when we'd be leaving this place."

"What do you mean?" the young soldier asked, turning back to face the veteran.

"Simple," he replied, "when we invaded Cambodia and surprised these fuckers, the North Vietnamese and Viet Cong didn't know what the hell to do. They fell back and we advanced, kicking the crap out of them. The next thing you know, public opinion back home forces the politicians to give in, and they announce to the world that we're pulling out by the end of June."

"So what's that got to do with anything?"

The veteran smiled, shaking his head. "There's maybe three good roads leading out of the country back into Vietnam, so now the enemy knows when we're leaving and how. So now, it's almost the end of June, and they know we're pulling out, so they're going to hit us with everything they have left. They know the time and place. That kind of information Mata Hari would have killed for!"

"Who's Mata Hari?" the young soldier asked.

The veteran smothered a laugh. "You enlist or get drafted?"

"Enlisted. Why?"

"Well, you would have done better in college. But cheer up, you're getting a good history lesson here. Vietnam— Class of 1970!"

Later, because of Hancock's information, the order was given to call in the fire support base's listening and observation posts. The NVA were massing for an attack, and the incoming mortars and rockets that followed soon after confirmed it. The NVA were advancing again.

# CHAPTER SIXTEEN

When Major Thomas Fitzgerald arrived in Vietnam for his second tour of duty, he wasn't too thrilled about getting stuck in a rear-area job in Long Binh. So he worked, finessed, begged, and cajoled his way into a combat position with the Cav.

Although positions in line units were often easy to find, those in the safe rear areas were seldom given up. So when Fitzgerald asked to be reassigned, he knew there would be someone eager to vacate a combat slot. The trouble came in finding a *good* combat position—if any position in combat can be termed "good." But Fitzgerald was a soldier, and soldiers fight wars. They don't administer them.

A month or so after his arrival in Vietnam, he got his wish when a position opened with "divarty," the 1st Cav's division artillery, and he lunged for it. Cannon-cockers are a vital branch of the combat arms, and he welcomed the opportunity.

It was while in divarty that Fitz, as he was better known, was also able to convince his higher-ups that not only did he have something on the ball but he was also a damn good cannon-cocker who knew what he was doing.

"With experience comes rank" is an old adage that isn't always the case. Many in positions of authority got there just by being in the right place at the right time. And although Fitzgerald would say, "I was lucky and maybe lucky enough to have good people under my command who got me where I was," those who knew him better knew he was also an accomplished soldier.

So naturally, when the division was looking for someone to take over the 2d of the 19th Field Artillery, their attention turned to Fitzgerald. Promoted to the rank of lieutenant colonel, the 38-year-old from Fort Edward, New York, found himself in charge of coordinating artillery support for the 1st of the 5th Cav during the Cambodia operation from Fire Support Base David.

He brought in six 105mm howitzers for the defense of the small base, which he was secretly convinced someone had put on the hilltop smack dab in the center of North Vietnamese Army territory just to piss them off and, of course, to draw their fire. Fishermen know that stratagem better as "bait."

But the newly promoted colonel wasn't about to let the enemy take the bait and run with it. Like shark fishing, hooking the fish is the easy part. The danger comes in trying to reel it in.

Fire Support Base David wasn't much to look at, nor was it all that secure. The barbed wire, what there was of it, was in short supply, and some sections that had been laid down couldn't keep out a wandering goat. Not that it was the engineers' fault; David wasn't designed to be anything more than a working laager point, a temporary base of operations for the Cav's role in the invasion.

Besides the grunts of D Company, the 1st of the 5th, FSB David also served as a forward post for divarty, as the Cav's 1st Brigade, and as a 1st of the 5th battalion rear area. Apache Troop helicopters laagered there from time to time, and a POL—fueling area—was set up to refuel the ships that were working the region.

FSB David's perimeter weak points were frequently pointed out by the enemy, who staged small harassing raids against it. One large-scale NVA ground attack had failed early in the base's life. In a predawn attack, the NVA besieged the east side of the outpost, taking out one of David's two large searchlights with a B-40 rocket before the first wave of enemy soldiers came up over the berm line. With his pistol in hand, Fitzgerald wondered what in the hell the noise was as he raced to see the enemy sappers desperately trying to overrun the American fighting positions.

Firing as he ran, he killed one enemy soldier as he passed unharmed through the exploding fragments of a grenade. Shoring up the holes he discovered in the line, Fitzgerald had his people bring up a tube and train the howitzer muzzle on the dirt-wall perimeter. Firing at point-blank range, the leveled cannon put an end to the enemy's assault on the eastern perimeter. Even as the cannons thundered, the main thrust of the NVA's attack hit the north side of the camp, only to be pushed back by the artillery men and grunts.

When the sun came up a century or so later, the fire support base had 30 wounded American soldiers. Enemy dead littered the countryside. One unfortunate enemy soldier, who had hidden behind a 55-gallon drum of fougassé, was sniping at the perimeter line until he accidentally gave away his position and the antipersonnel device was set off. He died horribly.

The attack had been at a cost that the enemy apparently couldn't afford. Future tactics would be chosen more carefully. The NVA fell back on sporadic harassing tactics of mortar and B-40 rocket fire. Though less concentrated than a ground assault, harassing fire could just as easily kill you as anything found in the large-scale attack. The NVA fell back to the standard methods of guerrilla warfare: pick at the enemy, bleed him slowly. It was up to people like Fitzgerald to make sure the NVA didn't succeed. And up until the night Ranger Hancock walked into FSB David after the ambush, the artillery commander knew they were still fishing and that the price of bait was going up.

The sharks were still out there, circling in a frenzy and waiting to feed.

# CHAPTER SEVENTEEN

"It doesn't look good!" Hugele yelled over the noise of the helicopter to Sergeant Beal, who leaned forward to get the rest of the story. The lieutenant's face registered his concern. The wise-guy sergeant was at Beal's right shoulder, straining to hear as well.

"One survivor at David!" the officer shouted, raising an index finger. "Just one! The base is on alert too."

The young officer was talking, but the Wise Guy was no longer listening. He swore quietly and shook his head, shuddering at his own memories of a LRRP mission he had been part of. Then, only two of them had walked out. He and the team leader, covered in dirt and blood and thanking God that someone had come to their rescue when they did, otherwise ... the Wise Guy swore again.

When the lieutenant had finished a brief account of the situation, Beal nodded and then passed the information along to the others in the helicopter bay. There was one LRRP alive and two wounded and hiding out, while the fate of the remaining two was unknown. Two more 1st of the 9th personnel were wounded on David from the incoming mortars. The stakes were rising.

It wasn't the worst-case scenario, but it could get that way. Within minutes, everyone aboard the three rescue helicopters and two supporting gunships would know the story, or pieces of it. The rest they would speculate on. There were many questions that still needed to be answered. What had happened? Why had only one made it back? Why were two hiding out, and how badly were they wounded? What was the fate of the others?

"Cochrane's team," Beal said to the Wise Guy, who nodded in understanding. They had known him when they were LRRPs with Hotel Company. He was a friend and fellow Ranger. There was nothing else to add.

A LRRP team getting hit was one thing. The nature of the job made it inevitable, the price one paid for being a hotshot LRRP/Ranger. Most LRRP teams had been hit or been in contact with the enemy at one time or another. Ambushes were something else entirely. Just as was missing in action, which made the mission a desperate matter of survival. Hide-and-seek with the prize being a life. Only one survivor probably meant that the team had escaped and evaded. It meant the team had been split and the others were on their own like Hancock. Whether they would be able to filter back through the enemy lines the way he had done wasn't even the question. They were seriously injured, which meant, at best, all they could do was hide and wait for help to arrive.

As to those who had died, if they were dead, the enemy would strip them of their clothing, remove everything they carried, and then leave them for the rescue force to find.

If the men were seriously injured, then the NVA might very well kill them as was their practice. But if they had survived and were taken prisoner . . . well, nobody liked to dwell on the possibility of the Rangers being in enemy hands.

Judging from the expressions on the faces of the others in the open helicopter bay, Beal could see the news was weighing heavily on their minds. In this war, it was easy to put yourself in the other guy's shoes because if you re-

mained in the LRRP/Ranger company or Apache Troop
long enough, sooner or later you would find yourself in
those shoes.

# CHAPTER EIGHTEEN

Leadership in combat is a lonely vigil, its cost measured in solitude and late-night echoes of conscience. It is never a popularity contest because no leader is popular for long to those he sends to meet the guns day after day.

Major William D. Harris, Apache Six, had the difficult task of commanding Apache Troop prior to and during the Cambodian raid. He also had the difficult job of following Captain Paul "Butch" Funk, a quiet but effective Montana native who had the distinction of being one of the finest commanders in the squadron's history. Well liked and a master tactician, Funk had earned high praise and honors upon his departure.

Harris would have to prove himself, and Cambodia would be his proving ground.

The division's AO, its area of operations, was over 3,000 square miles, with the troop operating 50 miles or more ahead of squadron or division headquarters. According to one military source, they were "thinly spread" over a wide range of enemy-held territory.

"Thinly, hell!" said one Apache Troop pilot when he heard of the description. "Most of the time it was like pissing on a raging forest fire. There were hot spots everywhere, and as soon as you turned to attack it, another would flare up behind you!"

During the raid into Cambodia, the troop operated for

well over a month from a makeshift addition to Fire Support Base Buttons, a mud-filled frontier boomtown. There wasn't much of a rear area to consider, and the daily routine seemed to revolve around each new mission. There was little time to rest or unwind, not that Buttons was the place to relax, anyway. Instead, the Song Be province outpost offered the aircrews and Blues a chance to catch a few hours' rest, a quick meal scrounged from someone else's mess facility or hastily put together by whatever element from the mess or cooking section had managed to piece together a field kitchen, and then back out for a new mission.

There was always a new bunker complex to check out, a new rice or weapons cache to recover, or a downed helicopter and crew to retrieve.

During that period the troop's aircraft took an extraordinary volume of hits, so much so that the troop came critically close to losing its fighting effectiveness piecemeal to the North Vietnamese Army's .51-caliber antiaircraft guns. The scouts bore the brunt of the onslaught, with the plastic and light metal frames of the small observation helicopters offering little or no protection for the two- or three-man crews.

Hovering at treetop level, they would open fire, purposely trying to find the enemy's positions and draw return fire. In this nerve-racking business, the scouts paid dearly, as did the Cobra gunships who'd accompany them. The NVA and Viet Cong would sometimes draw the fire of the scout helicopter only to pull the gunships into a well-laid trap where the large-caliber machine guns were well positioned to take them out.

What little protective armor they carried lay in the seat, which didn't do a whole hell of a lot of good for the gunship pilot or gunner since the attack angle for the Cobra was always feet first and body forward, hunched like a rider on a flying roller coaster.

"Just your average 'oh, fuck, we're gonna die' position," laughed one Cobra gunship pilot while explaining the attack angle. "There wasn't shit for protection because we were attack helicopters. Worse off yet were the scouts because they didn't have the guns or rockets we did."

Often what saved the pilots besides the gunships' massive firepower was the unusual and amazing flying ability of the pilots, who frequently pushed the aircraft beyond their specifications. Another pilot offered, "If you didn't push the limits, then you never really knew what you were capable of, and sometimes you had to try things just to save your ass or those of the people who were relying on you."

In the brief duration of the raid, Apache Troop lost more than its share of aircraft and crews to enemy gunfire. Those observation, lift ships, and Cobras that were downed and could be repaired were quickly patched up and sent back out. However, there were those that blew up in fiery explosions and fell to the earth with their crews still trapped inside. Replacements would take their places in new or refurbished aircraft, each usually aware of what happened to those who came before them. In the days before baffled fuel tanks, even a single round could turn the helicopters and JP-4 fuel into falling balls of flame.

The casualties were climbing with each new day into Cambodia, and Apache Troop had suffered its share of killed in action. First Sergeant Sparacino's list expanded daily, and its significance was beginning to show on his weathered face. As the unit's senior noncommissioned officer, he took his job seriously, going over the casualty lists and trying to figure out ways to prevent future losses. Was it equipment malfunction? Tactical mistake? Poor leadership? What?

When he had determined a cause—and not just the official cause—he set about to correct it. Losing men under his command in combat was not something he relished. Most of those kids were giving everything, and they deserved better, and as long as he was the troop's first sergeant, its *top* sergeant, he'd damn well make sure that they had a better than average chance at it. He knew war was not an exact science. There were too many variables. But he also knew if you took care of your people, their equipment, and their welfare—and not just on paper or with wasted words, but if you really got out there to see what and where the problems were—then you reduced the likelihood that those kids would be mailed home in rubber body bags.

A career soldier, Joe Sparacino knew the soldiers he sent out would go anyway; it was his job to see they had more than a fair shot at making it back.

The troop's aircrews and infantry reconnaissance platoon met the challenge day by day, outperforming even the experts' expectations and sometimes accomplishing what seemed like the impossible.

When crews or pilots were in short supply, others would volunteer. Even Apache Six, Major Harris, flew such missions and, on one of them, earned the respect and admiration of some who didn't personally like him. Not always well liked, in this case Harris' flying ability made up for what some considered his abrasive manner. According to one veteran gunship pilot, Harris might have been difficult to get along with at times, but he could fly the ass off a helicopter. He wasn't just good. He was damn good.

On one rescue mission, an infantry platoon had been caught in a bitter firefight on the edge of a North Vietnamese Army jungle stronghold. In the far reaches of the province and with no artillery support close at hand, the grunts were soon encircled, and the enemy was quickly closing in. With numerous wounded and the American platoon unable to fend off the continuing assaults, it was decided to try a hasty helicopter extraction, to literally pull them out of the battle before they were overrun and killed.

There was just one problem. There weren't enough lift ships to pull them out at one shot. The few soldiers who would find themselves still on the ground after the extraction would be sacrificed. According to one gunship pilot, Major Harris volunteered to take a small observation helicopter, a bubble-nosed Loach, to rescue those who couldn't fit in the lift ships.

With Jerry Boyle's gunship serving as its high bird, Harris took a scout helicopter out, flew the fast and maneuverable helicopter into the hot landing zone, and proceeded with the rescue attempt. On the ground and waiting as the small jungle battle raged, Harris held on to the controls as the grunts fought their way to the aircraft, dragging and carrying their wounded. Harris was unable to do anything to protect himself because flying the Loach into the shooting gallery took all his concentration. The Loach was a sitting duck.

As one infantryman scrambled into the back of the small open helicopter, returning enemy gunfire, covering his buddies and their retreat, it looked as though all of the grunts would make it.

A young soldier was yelling for another to hurry while he sprayed the thick jungle wall before him with rifle fire from his M16.

Still, it wasn't enough to stop the NVA from coming out of the tree line and taking aim at the helicopter. The situation was heating up, and with both hands on the controls, Apache Six could do little else but watch as the show unfolded around him.

In the gunship, Warrant Officer Boyle had just completed a pass and was pulling back around for another run when he saw an NVA soldier shoulder a rocket-propelled grenade to aim at the waiting Loach. The RPG's sudden *whoosh* as it was fired was drowned out by the whine of the helicopter's noise as the rocket headed for its target. Catching sight of the enemy soldier just as he launched the rocket, the young soldier who had been covering their retreat turned his attention and aim on the man.

The rocket hit the American soldier. The explosion took the soldier's head in an instant as Apache Six struggled to hold his position until the others were safely aboard. There was nothing to be done for the dead American.

As Boyle rolled in on the exposed enemy with rockets and automatic minigun fire, Harris pulled pitch and brought the shuddering aircraft up and away from the small, no-name battle.

"You didn't have to like him to see that he was a good pilot," Boyle said. "Or that he expected just as much from himself as he did the pilots in his troop."

Boyle, from Ventura, California, had the collateral duty as the troop's mess officer, a task that he attacked with the same intensity as he did the enemy. Maybe more. Boyle knew that Napoleon was right when he said an army moved on its stomach. It bitched about its stomach, too, for that matter!

At 31 years of age Jerry Boyle was the troop's real "old man," its oldest pilot. It hadn't been easy getting into the Army at his age, let alone into flight school, but he signed enough waivers to finally get accepted into the Army aviation program.

He didn't really feel all that ancient until he got to Vietnam, where he found baby-faced kids in loose-fitting No-mex flight suits jockeying half-million-dollar machines and swearing to God that flying in combat was "fun shit!" or at least "better than sex!"

Flying with some of those babies made him feel like he'd been born during the Ice Age. The trouble was the "babies" were pretty damn good! Ironically, Boyle had heard all about the Cav and the 1st of the 9th in flight school, long before he arrived in Vietnam. After he proved he could make the cut in the extensive and at times exhausting program, he was offered a piece of advice from a sympathetic instructor who saw what Boyle was going through.

"Listen, Boyle," the instructor said after handing him his orders to Vietnam. "You're a little older and wiser than most of these kids here. They think combat is fun. It isn't. When you get in country, don't volunteer for the Cav. They see too much action. It seems to be their trademark. Second, if you somehow end up in the Cav, keep away from the 1st of the 9th. They're recon patrols. The bastards are crazy. Got it?"

Boyle said he did, but when he found himself in country and assigned to the 1st Cav, he figured one out of two wasn't so bad. But then sitting in the officers' club in Phuoc Vinh (the home of the 1st of the 9th's squadron headquarters) awaiting orders to a unit, he didn't really think the picture was all that rosy. As long as he remained in Phuoc Vinh, the picture was looking worse by the minute. The cheap drinks in the small bar helped somewhat.

"Pilot, huh?" someone had asked, as the tall, red-haired Irishman turned to find a veteran pilot—a baby-faced warrant officer holding a beer. "So what do you fly?"

"Snakes," Boyle replied, thinking that maybe the veteran pilot was too young to be drinking a beer.

"No shit!" the veteran said, taking Boyle in tow as several other Apache Troop officers and pilots began to welcome in the new arrival. "We're always looking for good gunship pilots. So have you been assigned to a unit yet?"

Boyle shook his head. "No, not yet. I'm still waiting. Headquarters said they'd have something for me by this afternoon. Why? Who are you guys with?"

"Apache Troop. Up in Tay Ninh." The veteran pilot grinned, picking up Boyle's bar bill and adding it to the growing stack on the Apache Troop table. "We're just down here slumming with some of these peckerheads," the pilot said, motioning to the Phuoc Vinh pilots and officers in the bar. "If you're interested, we can always use a good Snake pilot. Besides, you don't really want to be assigned here with these assholes, do you?"

A major turned and scowled at the remark while the veteran pilot shrugged it off. "Sorry. These *gentlemen*, do you?"

Boyle shrugged. "I'm stuck here, I'm afraid. I can't just leave without an assignment. They'd have my nuts in a vise."

"No, they wouldn't. You can come back with us, and the troop can take care of the silly-ass paperwork. Congratulations! You've just been drafted!" the veteran said, handing Boyle another drink. When they finished, they said they'd help Boyle collect his things from the temporary housing billet. In the meantime, the drinks were on Apache Troop. "Fuck these other yahoos! Tay Ninh's about a 40-minute flight northwest of here. You'll like it, unlike these people stuck here."

"But don't I need an assignment?" Boyle asked. Not that he really minded, since that would keep him out of the 1st of the 9th, whose headquarters he knew were just a little over a hundred yards away from the club. Realizing the new guy's concern, the veteran pilot just smiled.

"Naw. One of our people is on the way to tell them you're with us. Besides, you don't want to stay here and end up flying for some dildo outfit, do you?"

"Nope."

"Good! Then, welcome to Apache Troop," the veteran said, holding out his hand as Boyle shook it. "The best combat troop in the 1st of the 9th!"

"What?"

"Apache Troop," the veteran pilot explained. "We've got the best combat record in the 1st of the 9th. Hell, we see more action than any of the other troops! Why do you ask? Have you heard of us?"

A sinking feeling began to grow in Boyle's stomach. "Yeah," he said. "In flight school."

"Must be because we're legends or something," ventured another pilot.

"Or something," Boyle said to himself as his new friends walked him out toward a waiting jeep.

"Gotta go. The jeep's stolen! To the flight line, driver!" he said as the others laughed, climbing in around them.

Five days later, flying out in remote Tay Ninh province, the aircraft in which Boyle was serving as copilot was shot down. The sleek Cobra gunship took two enemy .51 rounds to the controls, and the new Apache Troop pilot and his aircraft commander had to auto rotate to the ground. Shutting down the engine and letting the turning main rotor blades spin them to a predetermined crash-landing site, Boyle heard the school instructor's words coming back to haunt him.

Right after the impact, Boyle managed to crawl out to safety, and the aircraft commander followed suit. "Only 359 more days of this left," Boyle said to himself after the pilot asked if he was okay. "These bastards *are* crazy!"

And they were, too, earning the recognition and distinction few others could or would attempt to duplicate. After a while, even the new guys found themselves fitting in surprisingly well. All they had to do was survive the shootdowns, daily incoming rocket and mortar rounds, occasional predawn sapper or ground-probe attacks, the rats, and the poisonous snakes, and the rest was easy!

Several months into the war, Boyle found he liked the daily missions and even liked his collateral duties as mess officer, sometimes combining the two for surprise raids with his cooks down to division headquarters to "relocate" items for the troop's lean and Spartan mess hall.

"Hey! Where'd we get the steam table?" one member of the Blues said, surprised to find trays of eggs, bacon, and fried potatoes staying warm and fresh beneath the glass after one of Boyle and Company's relocation missions.

"You don't want to know," a cook replied. "Does he, sir?"

"No," Boyle said, looking at First Sergeant Sparacino, who had overheard the conversation from a nearby table. The top sergeant cradled a cup of hot coffee. "Eggs, First Sergeant?" Boyle asked while the top soldier woefully shook his head.

Mess officer was just another part of the job, like flying along with the others on the rescue mission in Cambodia, including Apache Six himself (as the copilot for Bill McIntosh), while John Bartlett, Tyrone Graham, Bill Fuller, and the others rounded out the aircrew. All crazy, he decided, and all pilots you wanted to have flying beside you when the shit hit the proverbial fan. It hadn't then occurred to Boyle that somehow and somewhere along the way he had become part of them, just as "crazy" and seen by outsiders in much the same light. All the 31-year-old Californian knew was that the flight instructor at Fort Rucker was wrong. The Cav was where you wanted to be in that war, and the 1st of the 9th had a strange way of making you feel at home. "Sure, I'm older than the babies," Boyle admitted to himself finally, "and maybe a little wiser, too. But I'm happy to be with these people."

"Hey, Mr. Boyle!" one of his cooks said, catching Boyle's attention after the mess officer had offered the first sergeant some warm eggs the morning following the "relocation" mission. "I heard there's all kinds of good stuff in Cu Chi like ice-cream makers, pizza machines, and everything the REMFs have they might not even miss, say, if someone or a few someones flew down there and managed to cart it off."

"Is that so?" Boyle said, considering the possibilities while Sparacino shook his head one more time and rose to his feet.

The cook nodded. "That's a roger, sir. The Old Man's gone, too, and won't be back until tomorrow."

"No problem. We could sneak down tonight," Boyle added with a grin, only to find the first sergeant standing directly in front of him when he turned back to the steam table.

"One problem," Sparacino said.

"We, eh . . . I mean . . . we're not really . . ."

Sparacino raised a hand. "Are you people talking about relocating government property. Is that what I'm hearing?"

"Well, no. Not really, Top. It's just . . ."

"Just what?" Sparacino said, facing the mess officer.

"It's just . . ."

"Save it, Boyle!" the top sergeant added, raising a hand again. "But if I was going to do something like what I'm hearing, I'd damn well make sure I wasn't wearing any unit patches, and I didn't get carried away with my mission. You understand my meaning, Mr. Boyle?"

"Yes, First Sergeant," said the mess officer.

"I knew you would, son. I just knew you would."

In Vietnam, there were always wars within wars, strategies within strategies. It was always a battle getting the things you needed to take care of your people, and quite often "small" violations of routine procedures were overlooked in favor of proper provisioning. Collateral duties and relocation missions were just side jobs, excursions, while the real war took priority. Apache Six, the troop commander, still had the headaches that went along with command, just as First Sergeant Sparacino had with making the troop function. Warrant Officers Boyle, McIntosh, and the others would eventually go about their other assigned duties. But that would happen later; for now there was only the rescue mission in Cambodia. It was the primary concern, and the day's necessary battle.

# CHAPTER NINETEEN

Because the South Vietnamese and American forces had plunged so far so quickly in the initial days of their raid into Cambodia, they met chaotic and sometimes hastily executed resistance. As the cynical NCO at Fire Support Base David had said, the enemy had everything going his way in the waning days of the raid into Cambodia. By then, when President Nixon had limited the depth of the push to a little over 20 miles, the battered Viet Cong and North Vietnamese began to coordinate counterattacks, trying to regroup to regain what they had lost or at least make the Americans pay dearly for what they achieved.

To deal with this threat, just as they had in South Vietnam, the Army established forward fire support bases to frustrate the enemy's movements by adding oomph to the attack in the form of fixed-site artillery. Pockets of resistance lodged in the broad expanse of jungle and rain forests. The concealed and defended sites were invisible from the air and barely accessible from the ground. There the North Vietnamese Army held on and fought back in earnest. If they had failed in their head-on confrontations with the Americans, they gained the Westerners' respect in the thick tropical rain forests. On the edge of the jungles and directly in the enemy's path were fire support bases such as David, which was designed to be an obstacle.

FSB David was one of those sore spots in the communists' side, a hilltop reminder of everything they'd lost. Surprisingly small, seemingly makeshift, the forward fire support base was something the NVA soldiers had to contend with if they were to regain the region.

Resting precariously on a small knoll, the grunts who occupied FSB David barely had time to set up adequate defenses before the enemy counterattacked. The perimeter was poorly constructed, not the fault of David's grunts or the engineers who helped build it. The war didn't have time-outs, and the constant barrages and ground probes kept those on David from gaining any sense of comfort or real safety or security.

Lying just behind the rolled concertina wire that was the base's actual first line of defense were claymore antipersonnel mines, which were placed forward of the fighting positions that formed its protective perimeter.

The antipersonnel mines, though, were a one-time-use commodity, and if the grunts didn't pay attention, could sometimes be turned to fire *toward* the defenders who employed them. North Vietnamese Army sappers, the specially trained infiltrators, made turning claymores their calling card.

To counter sappers, the grunts on David strung trip wire grenade booby traps and flares and even empty beer cans filled with pebbles, to ensure that the enemy infiltrators kept outside the wire. At David the ploy worked. But, where the sappers failed, enemy mortars and artillery succeeded.

When the Apache Troop helicopters touched down on the field outside the small outpost, the Cambodian countryside was surprisingly quiet. Too quiet. The fog was lifting, but slowly and laboriously. Morning would be slow in coming, if it showed at all, and the pilots had to use their instruments to bring the helicopters in safely. Sitting on the outside of the base didn't make any of the aircrews comfortable. But, it had to be done; the surviving LRRP had to be interviewed, his information being crucial to any rescue attempt.

"I don't believe it!" said the Wise Guy. He was staring across the base at a lone Huey helicopter that had somehow arrived before them.

"Who is it?" Cortez asked.

"Longknife Six, I think."

Colonel Burnett, the squadron commander, had touched down at 0500 in the fog, using an FM homer to land safely. These were his people, the LRRPs and Apache Troop, and if he couldn't get the support he needed from brigade, then he'd personally make damn sure everything was being done to support them. The determined colonel wasn't about to leave anything to chance.

The Blues Platoon leader, Lieutenant Jack Hugele, questioned the surviving LRRP while his squad leaders crowded around to hear the account and decipher what they could to plan the rescue mission.

Hancock was spent, and the situation report came in troubled phases.

"Where did you leave the others?" Hugele asked as Hancock tried to pinpoint the location on the map. The poor visibility and the confusion of the running jungle battle made the map useless, with one major exception: the location where the team had been inserted.

"We hadn't gone that far up into a bunker complex . . ."

"Where?"

"On a hill in the tree line," Hancock said wearily while the Green Beret officer studied the map in his hand.

"Where did the team fall back to?"

"Only three of us made it out of the bunker complex," Hancock said. "We pulled back down around here," he added, pointing to a spot on the map that showed grassland. "It's hard to say, a few hundred yards—but I know I can

find it again. If we just get out there." Hancock was looking around for support and found it in the Apache Troop pilots. But the fog was still an issue. Flying to David was one
thing because the pilots had high altitude as a safety factor.
The rescue phase of the mission was something else entirely. There wouldn't be the altitude buffer, and everyone
knew it. Getting in low enough to find the missing LRRPs
came after finding holes in the fog to locate the ground and,
of course, the jungle trees that towered hundreds of feet
into the air.

"Your call?" Lieutenant Hugele stared at McIntosh and
the rest of the pilots. Fighting the ground war was his responsibility, but the flying was the pilots' judgment call.

"Let's go," McIntosh said to Hancock. "You can ride
with me. We're not doing any good sitting around here."

"You're not serious?" a senior NCO from the fire support base said to the assembled Apache Troop officers and
NCOs, studying the sky, which was relatively easy to do
since there were only a few islands of blue in the sea of
gray fog. His people would make up part of the rescue
force remaining in reserve at David. But flying in zero visibility weather wasn't part of the bargain.

McIntosh didn't respond. He just smiled and strode back
to his helicopter, followed by Ranger Hancock and those
from Apache Troop who rode with him.

Hugele offered an assessment. "Looks like we're going
to try. You can hold your people in reserve. If we do manage to find them, we'll pull them out. If we hit any trouble
then you better be damn well ready to come in and back us
up, fog or no fog. You got that?" But the Blues Platoon
leader wasn't waiting for a reply. He was studying the map
for likely enemy ambush sites and taking last-minute brief-
ings from Burnett. They'd have the support, and Burnett
guaranteed it. Once again, the helicopters cranked, and
in the early Cambodian morning, the rescue force was

boarding the aircraft, checking weapons and equipment, locking and loading magazines into weapons, and charging rifles. One step closer, they knew when the battle came it would be a matter of inches to live or seconds to die. Combat is the world's oldest tragedy, and for the rescue force, the curtain was going up.

# CHAPTER TWENTY

On the flight to the remote fire support base, Warrant Officers John Bartlett and Tyrone Graham led the mission in the Cobra gunship, but when the three Huey lift ships took off in search of the missing LRRPs, Bartlett and Graham took up their standard covering position.

Taking the lead in the first leg of the journey had maybe more to do with restoring confidence; the second leg of the journey was tactical.

The rockets, machine guns, and grenade launchers made the gunship attack helicopter a formidable weapon. For this mission, it would be the lift ships' responsibility to scour the countryside, searching for the missing LRRP team, while the attack helicopters would lay back, watching over the flight formation and, when needed, scream down from above to cover them with a deadly array of automatic weapons. The NVA were often leery of any helicopter because of this tactic. They could never be certain whether the helicopter was alone or simply being used to draw them out. From time to time, they'd set traps for the gunships, but they had to do it very carefully because if the gunships encountered more than they could handle, then they could easily call in fixed artillery on the enemy heavy machine-gun site. Once out of range of the NVA's weapons, they could easily pinpoint the 105mm howitzer rounds called in from a forward fire support base.

More often than not, though, pilots like John Bartlett and Jerry Boyle preferred rolling in on the enemy locations. Some said it was because they were hot dogs or showboats; others knew it was because they were the closest support to any unit who desperately needed their help on the ground. Sure, they thought they had brass balls, and a few even swaggered from time to time. But maybe it was the job that made them that way.

John Bartlett was better known by his nickname Bloody Bart. He had more than 1,200 combat assault hours in Cobras. The 22-year-old Apache Troop pilot was a gunship hotshot, an attack helicopter ace. Many of the scouts breathed a little easier when they had him shadowing as their high bird. When the smaller OH-6 scout helicopters flew at treetop level to draw enemy fire, Apache Troop gunship pilots like Bartlett flew in lazy circles thousands of feet above, waiting for the chance to assist the action. These hunter-killer or Pink Teams, as they were called, formed the backbone of the aerial reconnaissance arm of the troop, not to mention accounting for the majority of the kills credited to the 1st Cav Division. That effectiveness lay in the hands of the young pilots like Bartlett, who made it seem easy. But nothing is ever easy in combat. Locating a target on the ground and then sighting in on it at a hundred miles an hour or more isn't easy, and when the enemy soldiers on the ground in fortified fighting positions are doing their best to shoot you out of the sky, it helps to have more than just a little bit of flying talent; you had to have nerve.

Bartlett had that, and multiple awards for heroism said as much officially, using phrases like "with total disregard for his own safety" and "gallantry in action." Bartlett had earned the acclaim and awards along with the Bloody Bart nickname for always staying in the middle of the fight, which came to be a trademark he shared with a handful of other pilots in Apache Troop. Most had been shot down more than once or had watched their best friends die in fiery explosions, so their commitment was always personal. Their collective attitude formed a collective bravery.

Ranger Hancock, who just the night before had barely escaped and evaded the enemy in a harrowing ordeal, was aboard the lead helicopter, ready to go back into the ambush site. His face was tense, something not lost on the rescue force accompanying him.

The lead helicopter would focus on the team's insertion point and last known position, and Hancock would fine-tune the search, retracing the team's steps from memory. The fate of the wounded Rangers lay in his ebony hands.

The weather was still dictating the mission. The fog was diminishing, but slowly. The ceiling was still ridiculously low, so the helicopters made do with what visibility they had. They flew low-level up a narrow valley with large, thick-branched trees lining each side. Wet open grassland, less than 20 feet below, blew back beneath the helicopters' passage as they thundered through the morning. Rounded hilltops peeked out of the fog as others disappeared menacingly in the loose gray backdrop.

Whenever they flew into the pockets of fog that refused to give, and those were frequent, the pilots switched to instrument readings, frantically calling out their headings. By luck, they avoided colliding into each other, hidden trees, and hilltops.

As they climbed to 4,000 feet, the fog gave way to blue sky and sunshine. Reassembling, the four helicopters took their bearings and once again looked for an opening in the fog. When they found one, they tried a different tack.

"Hang back in a loose formation," McIntosh suggested to the others. "That'll give us room to maneuver."

"Roger One One," the pilots replied while Bartlett and Graham said they'd take the lead and see how it was below.

Diving through the sky-blue opening, the attack helicopter went down for a better look.

To their surprise, the ceiling had lifted to nearly a hundred feet. It wasn't much, but it was enough.

"Bingo!" Bartlett yelled into his headset. "Bring the flight down. We have a break in the ceiling!"

"Roger, Two One," McIntosh said. "We're on our way."

Once beneath the layer of gray, McIntosh took the lead, this time using the terrain coordinates and dead reckoning as a guide. On track but running low on fuel, the flight made for an open knob 600 meters from where the LRRP team had been inserted for their patrol. They'd use it as a reference point from which to begin the search.

Contour flying over the initial insertion point, the helicopters moved on to the ambush site. In the area immediately preceding it and around the open fields, there were signs of recent enemy activity. The concealed bunkers and fighting positions were visible to the trained eye of the scout pilots, who had been forced early on to learn to recognize from treetop level the dull browns and faded, dying greens of old camouflage. The scouts quickly became familiar with matted bamboo screens, logged-wall bunkers, and old cover hiding entrances to underground complexes.

In this case, locating the ambush site was somewhat easy because even from the sky, the kill zone could be made out. Just as it was easy to see that the enemy had done a little searching of his own. Boot prints and trails were everywhere, the kind that suggested North Vietnamese Army regulars hadn't worried about who would come looking for the survivors in the foul weather. They hadn't bothered to erase their trails. They could conduct sweeps and searches and be gone long before the rescue party arrived.

"We moved there!" Hancock said to Blue, pointing to the area where the survivors had fallen back. Lieutenant Hugele relayed the information to McIntosh. Nodding his response,

McIntosh steered the Huey toward the point. The lead helicopter's crew chief, Art Dockter, trained his M60 machine gun on the bunker complex visible in the tree line.

McIntosh dropped his airspeed and flew slowly over the ambush site at treetop level, but little could be seen. What did catch their attention was the ripped vegetation caused by heavy machine-gun fire and explosions. The dense foliage and tree limbs blocked a more detailed picture, but what could be seen looked as though it had been through a shredder. But the shadows below concealed something more, something that would have to be seen at ground level to be recognized and understood.

"Movement! Left Side!" Art Dockter yelled, training his M60 machine gun toward a hunched figure coming out of the underbrush across the knoll.

One hundred yards away, Ron Andrus waved one hand at the rescue helicopter, trying to draw its attention. His other arm was too painful to lift but he tried anyway, carefully walking across the exposed hillside. He was hoping they'd see him, and praying to God they wouldn't open up with gunfire when they did.

It was a bold move on Andrus' part, but he had to try something. He could hear the helicopters flying around in the fog. Getting closer, and as it lifted and he lifted himself out of his hiding position, he could see them flying over the insertion spot.

"It's one of the LRRPs!" Dockter yelled, turning his machine-gun barrel away from the man.

"Take it down," Major Harris said to McIntosh, who brought the aircraft around and set it down as close to the ground as possible near Andrus' position.

"Shut her down," Harris said, taking McIntosh, Bartlett, and a few of the other pilots by surprise. The SOP was to hover near the ground and drop the Blues off before bouncing back into the sky in a running start.

Harris' order broke from the SOP, but then this wasn't a standard mission. There wouldn't be a second chance. Fuel consumption dictated as much as the weather, and the unusual mission called for unusual tactics. Even so, a few of the rescue pilots were disturbed by the departure from the safe routine. On the ground, the helicopters would be sitting ducks, their only protection being the 21-man infantry platoon and the helicopters' door gunners. Neither could stop enemy mortar rounds from disabling or destroying the flight in just one volley.

Bartlett said as much but was overruled. Shaking his head at the idea, he remained in his gunship, watching the Huey. Helmet on and monitoring the radio, he wondered when the battle would begin.

He knew it was just a matter of time.

# CHAPTER TWENTY-ONE

The two Rangers stared at each other for what seemed like eternity, and what went unsaid was transmitted in volumes. Andrus was in mild shock, teetering on going deeper, but elation and glee won out over his pain. Hancock seemed to find new energy as well. However, their adrenaline could only carry them so far, and they were both well beyond the limit for anyone, even Rangers.

"I told you I'd come back!" he said while Andrus nodded, staring back over his shoulder; back toward the hiding place. "I told you."

Andrus nodded and then turned back toward the Blues. "Clark . . . he's down there," Andrus said, motioning with a pained gesture to a small patch of underbrush. His wounds could easily be seen. The area around the collarbone was swollen and disfigured, dried blood crusted on his uniform. He pointed toward a line of dense vegetation. A purple-yellow cut ran the length of his wrist. "There are gooks all around here. We've got to get him," he said, moving toward the site as the rescue force hurried after him. His gait was stiff and slow, like that of a tired old man.

"Hold on," Sergeant Beal said to Andrus, stepping in front of the wounded Ranger and holding him back. "We'll take over from here. You just take it easy."

Several soldiers moved off in two separate directions to

search for Clark. The Wise Guy was surprised to see that Major Harris, the Apache Troop commander, was following Hancock's lead.

"I'll be a son of a bitch!" he said as the pilot followed the uninjured Ranger while Sergeant First Class Kenneth Yeisley—the acting platoon sergeant for the Blues on the mission—the Wise Guy, and Sergeant Beal went in the direction Andrus had indicated.

Yeisley was a career soldier who had carried a Browning automatic rifle until the weight of the weapon under the sweltering heat, and maybe the difficulty of tracking down magazines for it, made him go back to a more accommodating M16. He also had the annoying habit of playing his bagpipes every day in the rear area, which the Wise Guy said probably scared the enemy more than the damn BAR. But Yeisley knew his way in the field, and the Wise Guy and Beal followed his lead with confidence.

"Did you see that?" the Wise Guy asked while Beal shook his head.

"What?" asked Beal.

"Look who's going around the other end?"

Beal turned to see the major and one other member of the Blues disappear into the underbrush.

"Who's watching his helicopter?"

"McIntosh," the Wise Guy said. "He and Bartlett are staying with the aircraft."

"Good. This ain't exactly a secured landing zone. Looks like Blue is setting up a perimeter, so fuck it."

Beal followed Yeisley's lead while the Wise Guy covered him.

The point squad would find and secure a knoll overlooking the LZ while the rest of the rescue force took a tactical stance. Other helicopters were ferrying in more of the multiunit rescue force.

The Ranger Company commander, Captain William Car-

rier, who was also ferried in with the rescue force, was
studying the last known map coordinates the team had
called in.

A combat tracker team arrived a short time later, but the
area wasn't secure enough to let them work. The dog and
handler might be able to get a fix on the missing Rangers
if they could get into the ambush site.

Setting up protective cover, using the rolling hills to maneuver, Lieutenant Hugele had the Blues seal the area. The
platoon's medic, Specialist Four Richard DeValle, waited
with the main body of the rescue force.

The point squad, minus Beal and the Wise Guy, included Specialists Cortez and Bloor, who set up a
machine-gun position to cover the immediate area. Their
additional firepower and wealth of combat experience
gave them more than the high ground—something that
made the rest of the squad feel more at ease, considering
the situation. Bloor and Cortez were veteran machine
gunners, although on this particular mission, Cortez carried an M16 since he had been unable to procure a light
M60 from one of the platoon's assigned gunners. In combat, few people wanted to give up their weapons, especially on a rescue mission where contact with the enemy
could be expected.

Almost on top of the LRRP's hideout, the troop commander was surprised to find Clark well concealed in a
waist-high clump of elephant grass, hardly the place you'd
expect someone to hide, but then maybe the perfect location just for that reason.

"Over here!" Cortez called to DeValle, the medic, and
pointed toward the Old Man's position. DeValle quickly
moved in to assist the wounded LRRP medic.

Clark's leg wound was menacing behind the makeshift
bandage. He had lost a lot of blood, and his face was pallid

and drawn. Helping Clark back to the main body of soldiers, DeValle had his hands full.

"Doc, you might want to take a look at him when you're done," the Wise Guy said, gesturing to Andrus. The medic was rummaging through his aid bag for morphine and bandages. He looked up and saw that something was seriously wrong with Andrus.

"You okay?" Beal asked Andrus, who tried to shrug his response and failed miserably. "The team leader's down there," he said, pointing to the ambush site. "We got to get him, too. We can't leave him. Them," he added correcting himself, recalling the dead assistant team leader's face when he turned him over in the ambush site.

Talking it over with Staff Sergeant Burrows and Blue, the two point men quickly decided on a course of action. Beal took the lead as the rest of the point squad started to move toward the ambush site, a hundred yards to their front.

Meanwhile, Doc DeValle's assessment confirmed the Wise Guy's suspicions about Andrus' condition. He was seriously wounded. A bullet had ripped into his collarbone and bored deep into his chest without exiting. A preliminary inspection showed shrapnel wounds to his back and wrist, but it was the thought of the lodged bullet and the internal damage it must have produced that bothered the medic most. The medic suggested that Andrus be medevacked as soon as possible.

Andrus, by then, was going into shock, his attention span was slipping. He had been up for almost 24 hours, and it was a wonder he was hanging in at all. How he managed to walk was something even the medic couldn't figure out. If there was a mystery about Andrus' hold on reality, Sergeant Beal and the Wise Guy knew what it was—it was searching for the two remaining LRRPs that kept him going. Beal and the Wise Guy had both been

LRRPs with Hotel Company and had served well. LRRPs were like family—the team was everything—and until the remainder of the missing patrol was located, Andrus wouldn't surrender to his wounds. Period.

His concern for his teammates carried him over his pain. He wouldn't give in to the shock. He couldn't. There wasn't time.

"We have two Whiskey India Alphas," the lieutenant said, using the radio phonetic code to tell the brigade's temporary facility at David that several of the missing LRRPs had been found and that the two MIAs were wounded.

"We're going to check out the ambush site for any others," Beal radioed the platoon leader a few minutes later. The platoon leader told him to take it slow and stay close to the radio.

"You stay with the medic," Lieutenant Hugele said to Andrus, who still wanted to help.

"I'm okay, sir," Andrus said. "I can help."

The lieutenant looked to the medic, who shrugged, and then back to Andrus. "You can stay a little longer," he said. "But after we check the area, you're going out on a medevac. You got that?" Andrus reluctantly agreed.

Through the background noise on the radio, Specialist Jim Braun was calling in a medical evacuation helicopter (medevac) while Lieutenant Hugele maneuvered several squads around to cover the point squad's bounding advance.

As Clark was being helped back to the rescue helicopters by the medic, Staff Sergeants Burrows, Beal, Tony Cortez, Duane Bloor, and the Wise Guy cautiously moved forward, splitting their lead and approaching the ambush zone from different entry points.

Awaiting the next discovery, Major Harris, Captain Carrier, and the others would remain in place. The two commanders divided the responsibilities for a more complete and methodical search.

Meanwhile, the point squad did what it did best. The men moved toward their objective slowly and carefully. Up a slight lime-green hill, a golf course–like knoll, the squad paralleled a "runner"—a small, orange dirt path leading into a patch of jungle—and a fresh clearing generated by the NVA's ambush against the LRRPs.

Unlike the unsuspecting Ranger team that had walked into the ambush site, the Apache Blues point squad knew what to expect, but knowing the very real and probable danger didn't lessen the advancing point squad's apprehension.

Staying off the jungle path, they bounded into the kill zone from different directions, flanking directions overlapping their fields of fire in case the fighting positions were still occupied. What they discovered left little to the imagination.

The horseshoe-shaped kill zone of the ambush site was nearly cleared from the previous evening's small battle; the gunfire and explosions ripped underbrush and branches, exposing a battle site that smelled like a newly mowed lawn with just a tinge of cordite.

There were no bodies to be seen, and no one was visible. But that didn't mean shit to the Wise Guy or Beal, who had the task of being the first into the kill zone. Dark pools of blood lay clotted on the leaves as insects moved through them, tasting it before making off with the small shreds of flesh. The two point men had seen it many times before. Deep, arterial blood, more purple than red. If the team leader and assistant team leader had survived the brief but intense battle, then it would have been a miracle.

Pieces of equipment were haphazardly left around the ambush site: a Chinese canteen, one of the Rangers' M16 magazines, a hunting knife that had fallen off the Rangers' web gear.

The fighting positions surrounding the kill zone were empty, hastily abandoned. The rope ladder was nearly severed, hanging like a kite caught in a tree. The lean-to was collapsed and bullet scarred. Beal and the wise-guy squad leader crawled in and out of as many of the fighting positions and bunkers as they could without losing sight of each other or the rest of the squad. Their actions were naturally synchronized, a practice developed over the time spent together on point covering each other, watching out for anything unexpected, and knowing that the other would always be there.

With a keen eye and an M60 barrel surveying the wall of jungle to their front, Specialist Bloor oversaw their inspection, while Andrus, losing strength rapidly, was led back to safety by the medic. Cortez provided cover support for them as they made their way back to the platoon, then turned his attention back to the point squad.

Beal's rough-hewn face held a stern expression while that of the usually gregarious Wise Guy told Cortez and Bloor both that the search was useless. The two missing LRRPs were gone.

And, too, there was something more; something Beal saw that made him give up any hope as he studied the kill zone for any positive signs. A piece of an arm lay near an exposed fighting position. Beal shuddered in dismay. Quickly crossing to it, he saw the severed limb was unusually thin and yellow-brown. Vietnamese!

"Andrus and Clark were lucky they even got out," he said to Cortez, who quietly agreed.

"There's no way the others could have survived this," he added. The ambush had been costly on both sides.

"We better call it in," the Wise Guy said just as the first explosions rocked the quiet countryside, and enemy mortar fire rained down on the Blues and the point squad still in the ambush site. The sniper fire immediately followed.

The NVA were springing their next trap.

# CHAPTER TWENTY-TWO

Bartlett recognized the distinctive *whumps* from the enemy mortar tubes even before the first explosions began to fall in front of the Blues Platoon. Triggering the start of the attack helicopter, he was well on his way to cranking the gunship in motion even before the first radio report came over the air.

Through the excited reports and heavy radio traffic, he contacted the infantry platoon leader, whom he could see scrambling to get his men behind cover as the mortar shelling was followed by an enemy ground assault.

"Blue, this is Apache Two One. Over," he said into his headset as the infantry leader came back over the air in an instant.

"Roger Two One. This is Blue. Go."

"Pop a smoke and get your heads down!" Bartlett said as the engine hit 6,600 rpms and he nosed the gunship off of the knob, yelling, "I've got you in sight."

Specialist James Braun, the platoon's RTO, ignited a smoke grenade, and as the colored tumbling swirls rose ahead of him, Bartlett was back on the radio and rolling on his target, the screaming whine of the helicopter's turbine muting the small-arms fire.

"I ID cherry smoke. I say again, cherry smoke!" Bartlett yelled, confirming the location of the platoon's forward element as the red cloud generated by the marking grenade rose to the sky.

"Roger, Two One. Hit 20 meters to our front!"

"We're in hot!" replied Bartlett, barely airborne, as he started firing rockets over the heads of the Blues and into the NVA soldiers he could see coming out of the tree line.

Mister Graham hit the miniguns and automatic grenade launcher as they overflew the enemy position, diving off of the plateau toward the river below. Taking a hard left turn up a crease in the terrain, the gunship climbed back up over the lift ships still on the knob, their crews hurriedly trying to get the aircraft in the air.

There was a 200-foot ceiling over the helicopters but still less than a hundred over the NVA. Making another pass and in the 90-degree bank on the break, Graham started shouting and pointing to the muzzle flashes directly across from their canopy. The NVA were mounting an attack from two sides and focusing in on the gunship.

Bartlett yanked the cyclic back and immediately disappeared in the fog, so scared that he never even looked at his instruments. Holding his breath, he stared directly at the floor and slowly centered the cyclic. Twenty seconds later, they broke out of the fog and breathed a momentary sigh of relief. The battle below was still on, and the Blues Platoon still needed cover support.

"Coming in again, Blue. Keep your heads down," Bartlett said, finding another hole in the fog before turning toward it.

"Roger, Two One. We'll cover your exit," Hugele replied.

The Huey helicopters were lifting off of the ground toward Fire Support Base David as Bartlett and Graham made their second run. At David, Jerry Boyle had monitored the contact and the red-haired gunship pilot cranked the Cobra attack helicopter to life.

The quick-reaction force at the fire support base was being assembled to assist the Blues, who looked like they could use all of the help they could get. The small platoon was outnumbered and seemingly in the process of being surrounded. What the enemy did not know was that an attack had been anticipated, and that Lieutenant Hugele positioned his machine guns and crews in such a way as to keep the only possible enemy linkup locations separated. If the NVA were to make their plan work, they'd have to cross several open fields, and the platoon wasn't about to let them. Each time they tried, the raking fire from one of the platoon's machine guns drove them back. How long they could sustain the defense was another matter. Bartlett could keep the enemy back while the platoon held him in place, but it was only a matter of time before the ammunition would run out, and then the picture would change dramatically.

Frustrated by the defense, the North Vietnamese began lobbing in a second barrage of mortar rounds but missed the mark, the rounds falling in an erratic pattern. As the line of enemy soldiers held their position in a distant tree line down the knoll, a second line moved to flank the Americans from the original ambush site. What they didn't expect to find was yet another American machine gunner directly in their path. As the first mortar rounds fell and the NVA opened up on the rest of the platoon, the point squad maneuvered to cover their position and that of the platoon. When the NVA tried to flank the platoon using the small rise from their abandoned bunker complex, Specialist Duane Bloor bore down on the advancing soldiers, stopping them from succeeding. Bloor began taking intense fire as the enemy focused on his position, but the gutsy M60 gunner from Wisconsin held his ground as Cortez ran to assist him. "Thought you could use some help," he said, taking a covering position next to Bloor before firing his M16 into the nearby tree line where the enemy's gunfire was the heaviest.

Silhouetted enemy shapes in the distance now became bobbing pith helmets as heads peeked out to fire before quickly disappearing back below the ground. Sergeant Beal and the Wise Guy were busy holding back a squad of soldiers who were trying a run on Bloor and Cortez as the four-man point squad suddenly found itself cut off from the others. The open area of the grass-covered rise that was an obstacle for the enemy was their enemy as well. It was their platoon leader who'd bring them back safely, setting up a perimeter that allowed their protected withdrawal as the NVA pushed to reoccupy the kill zone. It would also be Hugele who'd direct the artillery battery on Fire Support Base David down on the advancing enemy after Bartlett and Graham had made their final run and had to break station for reloading. "Redleg Six, this is Blue Six. Give me a marking round at the following coordinates," Hugele said, going over his map as the Artillery Fire Direction Center on David coordinated the howitzer support.

Within minutes the *whump* of the 155mm cannon could be heard in the distance as a single round, sounding like a speeding car over wet asphalt, flew toward the enemy bunker complex and positions below. Just short of the target! Hugele adjusted the range and rattled off the new coordinates. "Give me an HE round a hundred meters west, and I'll adjust you from there," Hugele shouted over the noise of the battlefield.

"Roger Blue Six," the fire direction center said.

"Shot out," the unseen artillery man added, sending the second round down range. Within minutes, cannon fire was raining down on the NVA positions, firing for effect, as the

Blues kept their heads down once again. By then, the thinning fog was mixed with falling dust and debris from the mind-numbing explosions, blending in with the gun smoke and muzzle flashes. The air was dank and filled with the odors of cordite from the rifle fire, the JP-4 jet fuel from the helicopters, and the shattered trees and pounded earth. The senses were demanding control from a situation that was beyond it. Sights and sounds were wildly altered, and in the brief seconds of extreme quiet between explosions or helicopter runs, the sounds of the silence became memorable.

Lieutenant Hugele directed much of the artillery that fell on the enemy positions, which were becoming increasingly quiet in its aftermath. Huge craters were left after the artillery rounds sent dirt and debris skyward in brown clouds. Tree limbs were shattered by the impact and explosion of the artillery rounds—as was the NVA's will to attack. They had seized their first chance to trap the American rescue force and they had blown it. The artillery rounds falling on top of them and the American gunships pinpointing their own attacks caused their retreat. All they could do was withdraw to wait for another opportunity. The Blues had held their ground and suffered no casualties; NVA bodies were scattered over the rolling hills.

Sporadic gunfire from retreating NVA kept the battle from dying away completely. In the sky above, the helicopters were returning with the quick-reaction force from David. The rescue mission wasn't over, but the momentum had changed. They'd found three of the missing five LRRPs, but two were still unaccounted for and no one was about to leave now that they were this close.

Knowing the enemy was willing to put up a fight changed the complexion of the mission. The going would be even slower, the search confined only to controlled areas. When the fighting subsided after 30 minutes, they began their search again, the point squad taking the lead as the rest of the platoon moved in around them. The quick-reaction force from David covered the tree line below and the hundred yards of open field before them. Joining them was a group of volunteers from Hotel Company, the missing LRRP team's unit, who had made the long flight from Phuoc Vinh. Combined with the 15 or so men from the original volunteer force from Apache Troop and the platoon of grunts from FSB David, the Rangers brought the rescue force to nearly 50 men.

Periodic sniper fire hampered the search effort, making real progress difficult. The frustration was evident in the scowls on the faces of soldiers scattered over the area.

As the officers in charge on the ground hammered out strategy, the enlisted men wondered just what kind of cluster fuck it would turn into. They knew anytime you had two or more people in charge, egos were bound to be bruised. They were also aware that the NVA were still in the area, determined not only to fight back but also to press the attack.

The rolling countryside was deceptive, and the enemy used it to his advantage. The open fields and the pockets of rain forest that lined them gave way to large expanses of jungle that could and did easily house battalions of enemy soldiers. Fixed fighting positions and locations had been mapped out by the NVA, their coordinates noted and memorized. In the game of war, the Americans were the visiting team and the NVA had the home-field advantage. The game was far from over, and it wasn't wrapped up by a long shot. The NVA and the conferring officers knew it. If anything, the fight was still in the early innings. Like coaches and assistant coaches, the officers were deciding how to keep it from getting out of hand. There was no room for second place. No prize for the victors other than survival, and even that wasn't guaranteed.

# CHAPTER TWENTY-THREE

Even in combat there's time for reflection, and, although it must be brief to ensure survival, any comfort coming from it is often focused and intense.

Sergeant Beal glanced around at the faces of those in the point squad as he absentmindedly rubbed the bullet scar on the right side of his head. It was a subconscious reminder of an earlier time when those in the point squad had been enough to stop an enemy assault in its tracks and turn the tide of battle in their favor.

Just four people, but four good people he knew he could rely on. Sometimes that was enough, like that one specific day in the Dog's Head, that small spit of land in the far reaches of Tay Ninh that on the map took the appearance of a canine's face. A dog's head that was bordered on three sides by Cambodia and occupied by a battalion-size enemy force.

The point squad initiated contact by accident. They hadn't planned on it. In fact, the mission itself was to check out what intelligence said was an "abandoned enemy jungle bunker complex" a mile or so from the Cambodian border and to report back the findings. "A routine mission," they said.

Beal and the Wise Guy had taken the lead positions that day, walking a split point, and in the process somehow managed to slip just inside of the "abandoned" enemy base, only to find out it wasn't abandoned. The intell boys had fucked up. Everybody was home and hiding!

When the men of the North Vietnamese Army battalion heard the approach of the low-flying Loach scout helicopter, they retreated into their bunkers and underground complexes as they always had done. If they couldn't be seen and if they remained quiet, then they knew the Americans would probably fly away. At worst, the small helicopter would fire blindly down on the large jungle maze through the interconnected tree limbs and forest, but the logs and packed earth that protected the openings to their underground dwellings would hardly be damaged. Limited by fuel and ammunition, the Americans would turn their attention to more lucrative or lively targets.

What the occupants had no way of knowing was that this time the American helicopter was just flying in advance of the infantry platoon it supported. As the scout helicopter skimmed over the treetops, the Huey lift ships discharged 19 members of the platoon. Quietly, the point squad led by Sergeant Beal and the Wise Guy worked its way into the jungle and well beyond the guard bunkers protecting the jungle fortress.

Beal and the Wise Guy called in their find before checking out the first underground opening. There were fresh foot and boot prints everywhere; rice was still boiling in kitchen positions.

As the South Vietnamese scout that accompanied the platoon began to check out a fighting position that looked suspicious, the Wise Guy covered his advance from atop another fighting position. Within seconds the dark hole the scout was walking toward erupted with automatic-rifle fire as an enemy soldier, frightened at seeing his enemy so close, let loose a burst in fear. The first burst of rifle fire initiated a battle that was to last for hours and involve close-quarter fighting.

Within minutes, the enemy soldiers were up and out of their hiding positions, charging the point squad and the rest of the platoon in a blind assault.

There was no strategy or plan other than basic and immediate survival. Close confrontations gave way to hand-to-hand combat as wild small-arm and machine-gun fire hit targets less than a few feet away and struggles turned into wrestling matches.

Beal had just finished killing one advancing soldier when an AK-47 round grazed his head, driving him to his knees with a burning, hammering pain. A second member of the point squad, a new arrival from Bravo Troop, took a machine-gun round to his leg, while the Wise Guy was wrestling with another North Vietnamese soldier, wrenching the weapon from his hands and killing him before he could recover it.

All around the immediate area the enemy soldiers were trying to gain the upper hand by overpowering the smaller American force. When a two-man enemy light machine-gun crew and a third NVA soldier tried flanking the point squad from its exposed right side, it was Specialist Four Duane Bloor, Porky, who took them out with a long burst from his machine gun. Sure, he knew the continuous fire would heat up the barrel eventually and maybe cause rounds in the chamber to cook off, but what did that matter if you weren't alive when it happened?

The fighting was close and heated, and its outcome would be decided within the first few minutes. The point squad's resolve did the trick. The handful of enemy soldiers who had decided to follow the NVA machine-gun charge fell back wounded or jumped or scrambled back for cover as Bloor raked the rain forest over and over. As they retreated, Bloor charged up, firing short bursts with his 60, knowing then wasn't the time to lose the machine gun to overheating.

A veteran 60 gunner, Bloor kept the bursts short, eliminating another problem for its operator, that of running low on ammunition. A gunner could only carry so much ammo, and without utilizing short, effective bursts, he'd soon find himself out of ammunition, with only a useless weapon to swing at the advancing enemy. Like swinging a table instead of a chair in a bar fight, not only would it look ridiculous but it probably wouldn't work too well either.

The Blues had solved both problems by having qualified, competent gunners and a policy of requiring others in the four squads to carry additional machine-gun rounds. Unlike some units that gave the heavy gun to the replacements, the Blues subscribed to the theory that the 60 gunners damn well better know what the fuck they were doing.

It was suggested that each squad member carry a minimum of a hundred linked rounds to support the 60 gunners, but after a heavy firefight with the enemy, many began carrying an additional 200 rounds, not to mention a canteen pouch filled with grenades. The extra ammunition and explosives added a few pounds of weight to the Blues' web gear, but they were invaluable in battle. Those who bitched about the requirement before the sudden firefights candidly admitted it was a good policy afterwards. There was no more gut-wrenching feeling than knowing you were coming to your last few rounds when the fight was still on.

The Blues had gotten out of that firefight then, after a nearly two-hour battle that cost the enemy 39 dead and a number of wounded. There had been several "kick-out" resupply flights, where the scouts would throw out the 40- to 50-pound cases of 5.56 M16 ammunition or drop the heavier 1,500-round metal cases of the 7.62 M60 machine-gun rounds. Cases crashed through the canopy as the Blues fought their way to the ammunition, retrieved it, and then fought their way back to cover.

The enemy automatic rifle round that had hit Beal grazed

the side of his head, gouging an ugly blue-red trench the length of his head. Blood gushed from the ugly wound, and half of his face was discolored by a red-maroon mask.

Bloodstained and hastily bandaged, the sergeant from North Carolina continued to direct the squad, shoring up any holes in the immediate perimeter. Later he'd lead the platoon out to safety, stopping a second time to break up an enemy ambush farther down the trail while the Wise Guy covered his move, killing a sniper in the process.

Beal and Bloor earned Silver Stars for gallantry that day, along with Lieutenant Hugele, who directed the action. Others received Bronze Stars and Purple Hearts, and those in the platoon learned that they could rely on the soldiers around them to get the job done.

Rubbing the jagged scar, Beal felt confident with the squad and most of those in the platoon; they were good people all right. Still, there was always a price to pay for confidence building. A well-heeled veteran on his second tour, Ed Beal had taken part in numerous Cav operations up north, most notably the rescue and relief of the Marines at Khe Sanh.

In the Dog's Head, the point squad had managed to pull it off again, thanks to the rest of the platoon. With the support of the gunships and troop helicopters, they had kept the NVA from overrunning them in yet another no-name sudden battle.

The NVA's counterattack and flanking maneuvers were falling short of their objective, but, judging from their determination, the fight wasn't over. And judging from the way the officers were huddling over the map and pointing in several different directions and nodding, the next phase of the fighting was about to begin.

"We're going back to the site where the LRRPs were ambushed," Lieutenant Hugele said to Beal and the assembled squad leaders. "The quick-reaction force . . ."

"The grunts?" Staff Sergeant Burrows asked while the officer nodded.

"Yeah, they'll take the tree line down the ridge where the NVA pulled back, while the rest of the combined force will secure the knoll. You people did a good job at finding the wounded LRRPs," Hugele added.

There was nothing to say to that, so Burrows only nodded for the platoon, before shrugging and getting back to the mission at hand. "We after the bodies?"

"Yes," Hugele replied. "We're going to give it another try. From the survivors' stories and the point squad's observations, it doesn't look good, but we've come this close, and there's no reason to turn back now. If you want to rotate the point assignment, I don't have a problem with that." Hugele was offering the point squad a breather, but Beal and the Wise Guy weren't having any of it. Specialists Bloor and Cortez were pissed along with them.

It had to do with pride, and the lieutenant could see as much. "It's yours if you want it."

"We already know the area," Beal said matter-of-factly, his slight southern drawl making a quiet point. "We'll take the lead."

The lieutenant grinned and turned to watch the infantry quick-reaction force getting ready to move out. The gunships were making another pass, pulling back into the cloud cover for their attack angle. "We're going to come in on it at a different angle this time too. The grunts will secure the tree line and when that's done we'll move out. Be careful," Hugele added.

The quick-reaction force's platoon leader was informing the other members of the rescue mission by radio that they were advancing on the tree line. The muted radio traffic was laced with the squelch-breaking noise common to field transmissions. Squad leaders were checking weapons as the infantry officer gave a hand signal for the grunt platoon to move out.

Hugele hesitated momentarily, watching the grunts as they crossed the open field on line heading for the far woods. On line? *Across the field?*

Spread out at three- to five-foot intervals, the grunts covered a lot of ground. Of course, crossing the field on line made the advancing soldiers easy targets; something that wasn't lost on Hugele. Hugele wasn't alone in wondering what the hell they were up to; the rest of the Blues had turned their eyes on the formation. The Blues' standard operating procedure was to skirt open areas and work their way around to an objective. To them, the on-line advance was something alien, but reconnaissance platoons weren't like your average grunts.

"Sergeant Burrows, get the men down," Hugele said. "We'll wait till they take the tree line. I have a bad feeling about this."

It was an NVA .30-caliber machine gun that hit the two grunts closest to the tree line as the rest of the enemy force opened up on the thin line of advancing soldiers.

"Pull back! Pull back!" the grunt platoon leader was yelling over the battle as the line of grunts returned fire while retreating to better cover.

The radio was alive with requests for gunship support, but even before those had stopped, the Apache Troop Cobras were firing again on the enemy positions. Rockets were coming out of their pods and slamming explosively into the tree line as the gunships covered the infantrymen. Orange bursts from the woods returned the fire and were countered by the grunts.

"Keep your eyes open!" Hugele was yelling to the Blues, who had their own tree line to worry about. Sporadic enemy fire tried to draw them out.

The two grunts who had been wounded in the new ambush were still lying in the open; their cries and sobs hovered over the field between rifle bursts. While the grunts and gunships were trying to draw the focus of the enemy gunfire away from the two wounded soldiers, occasional automatic fire turned back their way.

"Oh Christ! They're gonna shoot them again," Cortez mumbled aloud, watching the wounded soldiers 50 or so yards away. One soldier's jaw had been severed, the mandible hanging as he desperately tried to push it back into shape. Sitting up with his feet outstretched and his hands helplessly holding his damaged face together, he was sobbing. The frightening cry carried across the gunfire.

The second wounded soldier's legs were splintered. He was lying on his back, writhing in pain, unable to turn and lift himself as enemy rifle fire kicked up around their position. They were easy targets.

"Oh Christ!" was all Cortez said as he looked at the wounded soldiers and then to Beal and the wise-guy point man. Putting down his M16, he sprinted across the open grassland in a broken field run toward the seated soldier. It was third and long for the wounded Americans, and Cortez was going for it all.

"Cover him! Cover him!" Beal yelled as the Blues laid down a wall of fire, giving Cortez time to bring back the first wounded soldier. It was an awkward carry, but he managed to pull the man up over his shoulder and pull him back to safety. Putting him down was anything but easy as the enemy gunfire tried to zero in on the target, to no avail. Cortez had made it back safely, and the Blues were laying down a blanket of suppressive return fire.

The black-haired, brown-eyed Californian was winded, with beads of sweat falling from his forehead. His sweat, mixing with the blood of the seriously injured soldier, made Cortez look like he might have taken a round through the shoulder. His chest was heaving from the run, but he wasn't giving in to fatigue. "Medic! Medic!" Cortez yelled to Doc DeValle, who was low crawling in his direction, before Cortez turned and sprinted back to help the other wounded grunt.

"What the fuck is he doing?" Burrows was yelling while rising to one knee and offering Cortez supportive fire.

The question didn't need an answer. Everyone knew what he was doing. Cortez was acting on emotion and instinct, and it was having a strange effect on all of those who were watching.

The grunts who had begun retreating were now back on line, swearing and moving forward. Two of their own had been wounded, and Cortez's courage had sparked something inside them as well.

What began as a slow, rolling anger turned into a full-scale assault as the grunts assaulted the tree line. The gunships only accentuated the attack as the Blues and Rangers joined in the battle.

This time there was little fire at Cortez and the soldier he carried, and when he slowly lowered the second man, he was assisted by DeValle and several Blues.

"Did we bore you?" Beal said.

"What?"

"What was that all about?" Sergeant Beal asked. Cortez was half bent over and struggling to catch his breath.

"They . . . they needed help . . ."

"Can't be Juan Fucking Wayne . . ." the smart-ass point man said over his shoulder before handing Cortez the rifle he had put down. "He usually takes his rifle with him wherever he goes. You forgot this, Tony."

"I didn't think I could carry them back and hang on to it."

The Wise Guy grinned at Beal, then back to Cortez. "Next time let us help, too, okay?"

"I hope to God there isn't a next time."

"You and me both," the smart-ass point man replied. He was looking over at the platoon medic, who was treating four wounded soldiers. In the distance, one of Apache Troop's lift ships, acting as a medevac helicopter, was coming in on a short final approach. Using his arms to hand signal the olive-drab helicopter to land, one of the Blues was acting as the ground guide.

"Could you give me a hand?" DeValle asked Cortez and the others as he helped the first wounded LRRP to his feet and started toward the waiting helicopter.

"Sure," Cortez said, walking toward one of the wounded grunts he had rescued. Gently reaching down, he helped the wounded soldier to his feet. In shock from his serious wound, he let the Californian guide him. Cortez carefully followed the medic's lead. "You're gonna be okay," Cortez said to the soldier, who wasn't listening. "Come on, man. You're going home."

# CHAPTER TWENTY-FOUR

Once the angry grunts had secured the far tree line, steps were taken to evacuate the wounded. The Apache Troop gunships were flying "stalking" patterns, waiting for the next round of fighting to begin, as the Blues advanced on the site where the dropped pieces of equipment from the missing Rangers were first discovered.

The going was slow. It had to be. Crossing back over the hundred or so yards of enemy territory required careful movement and maneuver, and the Blues' point squad understood the consequences of haste. Screwing up meant you died. Plain and simple.

Unlike the grunts who got on line and advanced across the open field, Lieutenant Hugele had the Blues Platoon move to the site by bounding up and around the bunker complex. As one squad moved, the others were in position to provide covering fire. When the first squad was in place, it would provide cover support for the squads that followed. This overlapping progress took time, but after witnessing the trouble the grunts went through, Hugele knew it was the best course of action.

Sergeant Beal and the Wise Guy were first in the enemy bunker complex, Cortez and Bloor following immediately.

Bloor, the machine gunner, set up watch while Cortez covered his flank. The two point men relied on their well-trained senses to serve as early warning devices and the alarms were already ringing—triggered by unusual smells not associated with the jungle, like the pungent *nuoc mam* fish sauce favored by the Vietnamese or the lingering odor of their tobacco that told the two soldiers the enemy had recently occupied the area. And there were the faint metallic sounds of equipment banging and bayonets locking, which confirmed that the enemy wasn't that far away. And the usual jungle noises—the screeching birds, monkeys, and lizards—were suspiciously absent.

When the NVA soldiers had dropped deeper into the bunker complex, they hadn't figured the 105mm howitzers into the equation, or the dead-center accuracy of the helicopter gunships. While the earth-and-log fighting positions were enough to withstand small-arms fire, they couldn't hold up against a hammering artillery barrage or 14-pound rockets.

Where bunkers had once been, the impact of 105mm rounds burrowing into the jungle floor had left humid brown craters in their wake. Back at FSB David, Lieutenant Colonel Fitzgerald's people were right on the money.

The treetop canopy—its weave of interlocked branches, dense foliage, and rope vines that had once sealed the floor from the sky above—was now open and torn like tattered, dangling greenery. Fractured branches were hanging askew, and that part of the enemy fighting complex, by then, existed in location only.

Any chance of finding a sign of the two missing LRRPs had certainly decreased. It would take more than the two point men and divided attention to find any clues in all the debris. The search for the missing Rangers was the Blues' primary concern, but a secondary and more ominous concern was the possibility of finding themselves in yet another ambush.

Pushing deeper into the woods directly behind the damaged site, Beal and the Wise Guy were frustrated in their efforts to locate the missing LRRPs. Signs of the enemy were everywhere, and dead enemy soldiers lay trapped in their small fighting positions, their bodies half hidden in the small collapsed earthen structures and half exposed in fragmented death.

There were also numerous footprints with no discernible pattern, showing that the NVA retreat was chaotic. But there were no LRRPs, no signs of where their bodies had been dragged to.

"Shit!" the Wise Guy said, frustration heavy in his voice. He shook his head at Beal as they moved in and around the area. Their search was becoming frantic because as they worked farther away from the entrance site, new fighting positions and bunkers were making themselves evident. It would take days to conduct a thorough search and a larger search party than was present. And that wasn't the main reason the two point men were worried. The size of the enemy bunker complex indicated enemy strength at company level, which meant the rescue force was outnumbered.

The persistent attacks the NVA tried against the search force said a great deal about the enemy's resolve. Neither Beal nor the Wise Guy would underestimate the North Vietnamese; they had bullet scars to show for previous run-ins. If they had learned anything as a point team, it was that these little bastards were tough!

"The gooks are still here!" the Wise Guy whispered to Beal, who nodded while studying the jungle wall before them. Farther in the distance, they could hear something or someone moving through the vegetation, short quick movements the way an enemy force would move if it were using cover and maneuver techniques. Branches and twigs were stepped on, and the distinct cracks reverberated through the underbrush.

"Any sign?" Staff Sergeant Burrows whispered as he joined the point squad.

"Not of the LRRPs," Cortez replied in a voice that was just as quiet as he leveled his M16 rifle at a bunker opening opposite the bunker the Wise Guy was searching.

The search was slow and methodical, and the strain was showing. Beal and the Wise Guy were frustrated because they could not track the missing Rangers. They expanded the search pattern as Burrows, Cortez, and Bloor moved in behind to cover.

The process was deliberate. You didn't rush into an enemy position as much as you entered it with a studied approach, the barrel of your rifle pointed at the edge of the dark opening as you angled your body to get a better look while still keeping the majority of it out of the line of fire. Several months earlier, the platoon had used a combat dog tracking team to find the hidden enemy fighting positions. But when the dog alerted on a bunker it had sniffed out, the handler bungled the procedure and was killed by an enemy soldier who was hiding in the bunker.

With his finger lightly touching the trigger, his palm squeezing the rifle stock, the Wise Guy inched forward, prepared to kill an NVA soldier who might be hiding in it.

The Wise Guy had seen it happen too many times. Hell, it even happened to him, and he had the bullet scars to show for it.

It was along a disputed border region of Vietnam and Cambodia known as the Dog's Head where the Wise Guy came across an enemy ambush in the making. At first, all he noticed was a single footprint where the enemy soldier on watch had turned away and walked back toward the rest of his group. The Wise Guy came across the footprint and stopped. His adrenaline was rushing as he suddenly realized he had worked his way to the edge of the ambush kill zone. As he looked up from the trail, the North Vietnamese soldier who was supposed to be watching the trail for the approaching Americans discovered the crouching soldier less than 15 feet away. The NVA screamed in fear and fired.

The first round caught the Wise Guy across the front right thigh, ripping the abductor muscle and sending the American sergeant falling backward as the rest of the rounds from the automatic rifle burst hit him a second time, tearing into his canteen, his boot heel, and loose clothing.

His left hamstring muscle was cut in half and bleeding heavily, but even as he was falling, the Wise Guy brought his rifle to bear on the enemy soldier and returned fire. Set for automatic fire, the M16 rifle sent 20 rounds back at the enemy soldier as the Wise Guy, in spite of the pain, kept his finger on the trigger. The NVA soldier fell dead while the Wise Guy scrambled to crawl for cover as he quickly reloaded. But his legs wouldn't respond, and they quickly grew cold and numb.

After being medevacked out to a field hospital in Tay Ninh, then surgery near Saigon, he would learn to walk again before he was sent back to his platoon. Learning to walk took a while, and learning to walk point again in the jungle was a slow process as well.

A new, more pressing fear accompanied him. It wasn't courage that brought him back or brought him out on this latest rescue mission, either. It was the realization that the missing Rangers needed help like the help he had received from the point squad when he was wounded. Besides, he had known Cochrane. Not well, but well enough to have a beer or two with him when he stopped by the Ranger company in Phuoc Vinh to visit old friends. When you placed a face to a name and remembered it kindly and when that person needed help, you didn't say no. Even at 20 years of age, the Wise Guy was smart enough to know that in life you often get through the hard times thanks to the efforts of a lot of good people around you.

Besides, the Wise Guy knew his business just as well as

Beal, Bloor, Burrows, and Cortez. Their status as veterans was hard fought and well earned.

"Be careful!" Burrows called, bringing the Wise Guy back to the situation.

The fog had long since given way before the afternoon sun, but the day was now giving way to dusk. Sunset was still hours away, but the rescue force was milking the day for as much light as it would give.

A radioman moved up to join Burrows, passing him the handset. From Burrows' face, it wasn't good news.

"The high bird's got enemy movement everywhere. It seems they're coming out of the woodwork."

"Fuck 'em," Cortez said, while Burrows laughed and shook his head at the response.

"You did good out there. The wounded grunts, I mean."

"They needed the help," Cortez said, surveying the jungle.

"Yeah, but you seemed to be the only one who did anything about it," said Burrows, who was surprised to find that the Mexican-American was shaking his head.

"That's bullshit, and you know it. I wouldn't have gone if I didn't think our guys would cover my ass. I was just the first one to them. That's all." There was some truth to what the specialist four was saying. The platoon had its share of individuals whose collective bravery drove them forward in combat even when their common sense told them it would be safer to remain where they were. It had little to do with macho or heroics but was more a matter of duty and honor. The platoon's job was rescue and reconnaissance, and even when the men were frightened by the war around them, they still carried out their mission. Sometimes they did more. Burrows knew better than to argue with Cortez, and he was beginning to think that maybe it was something to do with the point squad.

Cortez didn't know that earlier, during a lull in the fighting when there was time to assess the damage, check ammo and weapons, light up a badly needed cigarette, and figure out when the enemy might try again, a grunt sergeant had made the mistake of downplaying Cortez's one-man rescue in front of a few Rangers from Hotel Company: Staff Sergeant Burrows, Beal, and the Wise Guy. The barrage of insults aimed at the grunt sergeant hit their target. Surprisingly, one of the most vocal was Staff Sergeant Burrows. "He did what everyone else wanted but was too fucking scared to do!" he said, standing over the critic with his blunt face coloring and threatening enough to underline the point.

"You ever think about making the Army a career?" Burrows asked Cortez, who turned away from the jungle to see if Burrows was kidding. Right in the middle of Cambodia with gooks all around them, and there's Burrows giving him a fucking reenlistment pep talk.

"You suffering from heatstroke or what?" Cortez said, turning back to his sentry duty.

The staff sergeant caught Bloor's smile at the exchange. "Me neither," Bloor said. Yeah, Burrows decided. It was definitely something with the point squad. Good soldiers, but definitely they were all fucking wise guys.

# CHAPTER TWENTY-FIVE

The Ranger Company commander didn't want to give up the search, but time and circumstances were working against him. Those were his people out there, and he wasn't about to give up on them. The anguish on his face said as much.

He wasn't getting any argument, but everybody with any say was making his view known. Daylight was the primary concern. The enemy occupied the area of operations, and it was his backyard. If he was tenacious with the sun up, then he'd be hell to contend with through the night. In the open, the NVA could easily walk mortars in on the American positions. Coupled with the fact that the gunship support would be lost to the darkness as well, and that the enemy outnumbered them, the picture was anything but rosy.

It was believed the team leader and assistant team leader had been killed in the initial ambush. However, until their bodies were recovered, there would be no way to know for certain. But finding the missing Rangers, or their bodies, was proving to be a difficult task. If they had somehow managed to survive, which seemed more unlikely as the situation unfolded, then they might have been quickly moved out of the area to an underground field hospital and treated. If they were dead, then the Vietnamese might very well have moved the bodies out of the area, just to bury them away from the bunker complex; dead, decomposing bodies were a health hazard, not to mention that their presence would have made the living area very unpleasant.

Arguments were springing up among the various platoons of the combined rescue force, although the conversations were not so much heated as they were concerned.

"The gooks don't take EM [enlisted men] prisoners," one member of the Blues said. "They go for the technical shit—the pilots and officers—because of their public relations or military value."

"Yeah, but they were LRRPs!" someone else countered.

"So? If the rumors about the bounty on them are right, then their value dead or alive is the same. Besides, if they were seriously wounded . . ." The soldier let it trail. Everyone in the platoon knew what he was going to say; they had seen it too many times on helicopter rescue operations, they would arrive only to find the injured crew members had been machine-gunned in their positions. The LRRPs' rucksacks with their code book and SOP book, emergency-frequency radios, and maps were nowhere to be found. Dropped and left in the kill zone during the ambush, there was no reason to believe they hadn't been discovered and whisked away for their intelligence value. During the sweeps of the ambush site and area immediately surrounding it, with the exception of several loose pieces of nonessential equipment, the Apache Troop Blues couldn't locate the rucksacks. The real question was where did they go? Answering that was the job of the point squad, but they were coming up empty. The reaction force needed more time and a larger search pattern.

"No sign of them. Nothing," the Wise Guy said to Burrows as Sergeant Beal echoed his report. "Just blood trails, dead NVA, and a lot of movement out there."

"Where's the movement? Which direction?" the staff sergeant asked.

"Everywhere," the Wise Guy said; he wasn't joking.

"They're holding back, but they're out there. Waiting," he added as an afterthought.

"They're not doing anything to hide their trails either," Beal added. "They're everywhere."

"That's what the gunships are saying, too," Burrows said. "Christ! They're not about to let us recover the bodies. They know we'll keep looking and trying. That's their only ace." It was true, but it was something the others didn't care to admit. Apache Troop's policy was to recover all American bodies—all friendly KIAs. Nobody got left behind. Ever. And their recovery record was more than just something to take pride in. It was something they could rely on, knowing that if they were to fall into similar circumstances, then they'd get pulled out, too. Leaving anyone behind was unsettling, and the strain was beginning to show.

"Try one last search but don't move out too far and don't get separated," Burrows said as Sergeant Beal and the Wise Guy turned their attention to another section of the extensive bunker complex, dividing up the area between them and going about their work.

Beal and the Wise Guy were a split point team—they'd cover each other as they moved, one taking a momentary lead while the other covered the movement before alternating the responsibilities. The two had even managed to earn a reputation for their abilities. They were good at their jobs, good at their work, which they viewed professionally, while others viewed it as just plain asking for trouble. Walking point, they knew, was easy and dumb. All anyone had to do to be successful was simply move ahead of the platoon and draw the enemy's fire, and if he survived, do it all again on the next mission. Point men usually didn't last long on their jobs, but Beal and the Wise Guy had made it their specialty.

Each had been hit by enemy automatic rifle fire walking

point; Beal with a grazing bullet wound to his head, the Wise Guy shot in both legs breaking up an enemy ambush directed at the platoon. They became good at their jobs out of necessity, and they trusted each other implicitly. They also trusted those in the squad to assist them when they did draw enemy fire. On point, getting out of trouble was a hell of a lot more difficult than getting into it. When the shit hit the fan, it was good policy to have someone around who knew how to cut the power. Smart policy.

Although the two buck sergeants were gung ho, they weren't necessarily stupid. "Glad you're here, Porky. Really glad," the Wise Guy said to Bloor, the machine gunner, who only smiled. "Him, too," the Wise Guy threw in for Cortez's sake. "If I get shot and Juan Wayne here puts his rifle down in the dirt again, then you have my permission to drop him for push-ups."

"You, I'll leave," Cortez snickered. Burrows watched the exchange wondering how 20-year-olds ever got to become sergeants anyway. The Wise Guy had become a sergeant at 19; something which left Burrows shaking his head even if he admired the smart-ass for the job he did. Half the men of the platoon were wet behind the ears, but they were all swimming like pros. Who could figure?

"Ten minutes," Burrows said to Sergeant Beal, holding out two outstretched hands wide open and mouthing the words so the meaning wasn't misunderstood.

"Ten!" The quiet Southerner nodded once before moving out with the Wise Guy to begin their next search pattern. As the enemy began feeling his way back into the battle, sporadic rifle fire broke the silence, but none came toward or from the ambush site. Beal and the Wise Guy moved quietly, and perhaps that explained it. Too, maybe the NVA were just drawing them in. The occasional rifle shots were enough to jolt the men of the point squad, who dropped into better defensive positions with each enemy round fired. The search was going slow and with little results.

"Hold up!" Burrows said, drawing Beal's attention as the Wise Guy began to enter another empty enemy fighting position. Empty shell casings were everywhere, indicating that the NVA had used them in their ambush and attack. The separate pools of AK-47 casings and M16 shells told the story of the firefight. But still, there was no sign of the two missing Americans.

The main body of the combined rescue force was concentrating on keeping the immediate operational area secure. The task, which seemed to be taking them farther away from the kill zone, wasn't going unnoticed by the Blues' point squad. "Where in the hell are they going?" Cortez asked as he watched the soldiers move down a wet grassy slope toward still another tree line.

"What?" Burrows said, turning his attention to Cortez and then back to the direction he had indicated with his own focus.

"The quick-reaction force! They're moving in the wrong direction. The LRRPs were hit here. If we're going to find them anywhere, it'll be here or the ravine just down the gully to our right," Cortez said. A thin ravine skirted the small, wooded bunker complex and formed a natural avenue of escape.

"They're trying to push back the NVA. It's like we disturbed an ant mound," Burrows explained. "If they pull in behind us, then they'll be all over us, and we'll be up the proverbial creek."

"But it's open field for the most part. Can't the gunships keep whoever's in the tree line back? That would give us more people to do the search here." It was a logical question, but combat seldom fell within the realm of logic.

"Not our decision," Burrows said finally.

"Then how in the fuck are we supposed to find them?"

"We do what we can."

Cortez caught the Wise Guy's attention with two finger snaps and pointed toward the ravine. With a hand signal system, Cortez let the Wise Guy know he'd check out the ravine if the Wise Guy and Beal would follow him. The Wise Guy nodded and so did Beal.

"They're calling us back," Burrows said, interrupting the attempt. "Wrap it up! Wrap it up!" Burrows said again, listening to the radio while motioning the two point men back. "They're calling for an extraction. Looks like we're getting out of here."

"What about the missing Rangers?" the radioman asked while Burrows and the others stared at him.

"Missing in action," Burrows said, his voice and demeanor taking a noticeable drop. It bothered him to say as much; as a professional soldier and Army lifer, the words didn't come easy. "Call it in," he said, "and then prepare to move back to the platoon. Cortez, you take the lead." When Sergeant Beal and the Wise Guy returned, he said, "And you two bring up the rear. We don't want any surprises. Specialist Bloor and I will follow Cortez and the RTO. Any questions?"

"Yeah." It was the RTO. "We won't leave the bodies? We'll come back, right?"

"I hope to God somebody does," Burrows said before motioning to Cortez. "Move out and keep your distance. Got it?" The soldiers nodded their response as their attention returned to the sounds of movement farther into the jungle. The NVA were filtering back into position, taking their time, while the point squad and the rest of the rescue force prepared once again to meet them. The North Viets weren't about to rush because as the day wore on, they knew their time was coming. They'd pick at the Americans and harass them, and when the opportunity presented itself again, they'd mount another attack. Two thousand years of war had taught them to be patient.

# CHAPTER TWENTY-SIX

The open bay of the Huey helicopter was awash with streams of vibrating blood as it dripped from the field dressing bandages, mixed on the aluminum floor, and then flowed toward the edge of the chopper's cargo area where it was caught by the air currents and hurled against the recessed areas of the aircraft and tail-boom section. The boots and flight suit pant legs of the crew chief and door gunner were sprayed maroon with blood.

Aboard the medical evacuation helicopter, the Army medic, a worried, thin-faced spec four, had his hands full caring for the four wounded. Three were seriously wounded and could die before reaching the field hospital. The signs were all there—gaping wounds, splintered bones, and deep red arterial blood. Pale faces and cold extremities indicated that shock was settling in. The pilot knew the score because the crew medic was filling him in as he worked among the wounded soldiers. They were an air ambulance heading toward the closest field hospital, balls to the wall.

The pressure in Andrus' chest was building, and he felt hot and dizzy again, the effects of an unchecked infection stemming from a gunshot wound. The Indiana native was exhausted, not quite literally drained, but he had lost more than enough blood to qualify for runner-up. His mouth was dry, as were his chapped and splitting lips. When he swallowed, everything tasted metallic, another result of his wounds.

He felt a mix of elation and very real dread—joy at being alive but gutted by the thought of not being able to do anything for his team leader. Survivor's guilt was slowly taking hold of the wounded LRRP, and the anguish was as great as the pain of his injuries, leaving him cold and numb. Dying was easy. Surviving and remembering seemed to be the real struggle.

As the blood flowed over the helicopter floor and the medic went from patient to patient checking seat belts and bandages, Ron Andrus started to laugh. A cough really. LRRPs usually rode on the edge of the helicopter bay with their feet on the skids. He couldn't remember when he had used a helicopter seat. Let alone a seat belt!

A bullet had passed through Andrus' collarbone and lodged somewhere in his chest, and he sustained searing shrapnel wounds to his right wrist and upper back from grenade fragments in the ambush. He'd been missing in action for an emotional eternity and run through the combat wringer a few more times before finally being pulled out. And the medic had buckled him into the seat for safety!

The war was proving to be an absurd roller coaster of highs and lows. Stuck on a 365-day ticket, the Indiana Ranger knew you simply hung on and took each twist and turn as it came. Whether you laughed or cried, the momentum still pulled you forward.

The medic was working on Andrus now, and he was fading in and out of consciousness. He hadn't felt as though he'd lost a lot of blood, but he had three open wounds.

"You're gonna be okay," the medic said to Andrus before going on to the next patient. "Hang in there. We're almost there."

The pat answer was one that most medics used on their patients. It sprang from the theory that if you thought you were okay then you would be okay. It was something learned during previous wars when wounded soldiers with nonlethal wounds feared the worst and their bodies responded. Simply put, they died because they believed they were dying.

"Shock," the medics were told in their medical training at Fort Sam Houston in Texas, "could do funny things to people. If you're in a bad firefight and you have more wounded than you have morphine, then you carry some M&Ms or mints and you convince the wounded they're pain pills. And you know what? They'll believe you!"

"You know what else?" the soon-to-be combat medics were asked. "Their minds will shut down the pain because they believe it. The psychological assists the physiological."

Andrus had lost all track of time, not that it mattered anyway. As he glanced out of the helicopter, judging from the size and number of military buildings, equipment, and guard posts, he realized they were coming into a large rear-area logistics center. The infrequent metal-roofed structures gave way to a discipline of buildings and military colors; olive drabs and worn, sun-weathered browns.

The Huey slowed, then hovered to a stop as medics, nurses, and doctors raced out to the helicopter and took charge of the wounded.

Andrus was unbuckled and quickly lifted to a stretcher, then hurried through a series of swinging doors of the combat emergency room of the 93d Field Hospital in Long Binh. Within minutes, his tattered uniform was cut away. He was X-rayed and prepped for preop—the emergency surgery to close up any wounds that could be life threatening.

When that was accomplished and the surgeons had had time to assess the damage, he'd be wheeled into a large, factory-like surgery room where the doctors could operate to get the bullet. To do that they'd cut open his chest, shore up the jagged tunnel the enemy machine-gun round had made, and trace the path to the jacketed bullet that, as it turned out, lay barely an eighth of an inch from a major artery.

A needle was inserted into his arm, and plastic tubes were carefully readied to drain his lungs. The sodium pentothol did its job, and within seconds he was unconscious. Long before he came to and learned the full extent of his injuries, the doctors had already cleaned up and decided his fate over coffee with the radiologist. The wounded LRRP/Ranger would be sent to Camp Zama, Japan, to recover before being sent home. Recovery would be slow. Painful. Vietnam was the emergency room for the seriously injured, and the swinging doors seemed to be stuck in the open position.

It was all bad business, and business was good.

# CHAPTER TWENTY-SEVEN

"We're going back in," McIntosh said to Harding, who was checking out the tail boom of the helicopter, looking for bullet holes while Art Dockter was restocking the door gunners' positions with ammunition. Dockter struggled under the weight of the heavy, rectangular 1,500-round metal cases, using his knee as well as his arms to wrestle them up and into the well.

"They find the others?" Dockter asked. The pilot frowned and shook his head. "No, but the gunships are reporting gooks all over the place. We're going back in to get them out of there."

"Crank them up!" someone yelled to the other two lift ships while one of the other pilots nodded, circling his right hand in short, fast movements to his crew who were talking with grunts on a nearby perimeter bunker. They got the message.

Outside of the ships, a few of the resting pilots and crew members gave McIntosh a thumbs-up as the rest of the lift-ship contingent headed toward their aircraft from the makeshift command center.

The Apache Troop commander, Major William Harris, was busy coordinating the operation, which was changing by the moment.

Back along the rolling hills of the ground-combat site, Lieutenant Jack Hugele, Blue, was busy as well, setting up the platoon to serve as the security for the grunt quick-reaction force. They would be the first to be extracted or lifted out of the pickup zone, along with the volunteer force of Rangers from Hotel Company. It was an unofficial policy that the unit requesting the assistance be the last out, while those who came in to assist would be the first to go.

The quick-reaction force was in position. The grunts were separated by squad and spread out with enough distance between them to accommodate a safe extraction. Of course, "safe" depended largely upon the enemy. If they charged the helicopters, they might be able to blow one up before the Blues and the gunships could cut them down. Of course, the NVA might just wait and hit them with mortar rounds, or they might let the grunts go first and hit the Blues on their way out when cover support would be minimal.

Waiting for the first lift of extraction helicopters, the Americans covered the surrounding countryside, looking for anything out of the ordinary. Any movement at all. They weren't about to be caught off guard or be unaware of the enemy's tactics again. The LRRP/Rangers' ground posture was similarly cautious, but then they weren't used to being in the field with such a large force. Neither were the Blues, who usually went out with from 17 to 21 men. Perhaps it was the grunt quick-reaction force that felt the most vulnerable since they were used to being out with a company, from 90 to 120 men. They were the ones who appeared the most apprehensive, while the Blues and the Rangers seemed to take it in reasonable stride.

Ranger Johnny Rodriguez joined the point squad to offer his thanks along with several LRRPs whose faces neither Sergeant Beal nor the Wise Guy recognized. The war was constantly changing and so, too, were the players. When Beal and the Wise Guy were with Hotel Company, the faces seemed older, wiser maybe; many of the newer replacements seemed painfully young. But then, had they looked at their own faces five to six months earlier, they wouldn't have been that much different from the new guys.

In the distance, the first lift of helicopters could be heard chopping its way through the afternoon sky as Rodriguez and the point squad said their good-byes.

"You the one that saved the grunts?" Rodriguez asked. Cortez nodded.

"You got balls," Rodriguez said, shaking the hero's hand before making his way back to the Rangers' staging area.

There was some concern about staying to find the two missing LRRPs. The original plan was to pull the Blues out and leave the Ranger Company personnel and the grunts from David to find them, but that decision was overridden by higher-ups. The grunts and the Rangers would be pulled out as well; the site was too hot to leave anyone behind.

The grunts from Fire Support Base David who had been ferried in to continue the search were now being assembled for evacuation.

"I thought the grunts were going to stay?" the Wise Guy asked Beal, who shrugged.

"I think maybe someone realized it would be too dangerous. Too costly," Beal said. The Wise Guy remained surprisingly quiet.

"They're there. I know it," Cortez said, looking back toward the ambush site. "Jesus, I wish we could have found them."

"We all do, Tony," the Wise Guy said. "But the gooks aren't about to let us. There's nothing we can do. Come on. We got to go."

The extraction would be hot, which meant those covering the pickup zone would fire into the tree line to keep the enemies from even thinking about sticking their heads out to see what was going on. The helicopter's door gunners would begin the firing, then those on the ground would join in, aiming at the most obvious areas the enemy could attack from—the known bunker and fighting positions, the small paths and runners, even the areas of dense vegetation in which it would be easy for an enemy soldier to hide with a shoulder-fired rocket.

The Cobra gunships were zeroing in on a few targets of their own, while the radio cackled with traffic.

When the first lift was extracted and the grunts safely on their way, the Rangers moved into position for their lift out. The pattern of supporting gunfire echoed for the outgoing Rangers as well, until the Blues were the last to remain. The outgoing rifle fire was decreasing while the incoming was rapidly building in intensity. The NVA were still some distance away, moving through a distant tree line, their return fire sporadic and unfocused.

"Ever feel like those dumb shits at the Alamo?" the Wise Guy asked Beal when the RTO reported the helicopters were taking return fire and the NVA were closing in on the pickup zone.

"Me and Davy Crockett!" Beal said, checking the magazines he had remaining in his ammunition pouches and hoping the NVA wouldn't attack in full force. There wouldn't be time for a kick-out of ammunition, let alone time to reload magazines. Whatever was left would have to be enough. He switched the M16's selector switch from automatic to semi, which meant every time he pulled the trigger his rifle would only fire one round.

The automatic setting would be used for close-in fire when there wasn't time to keep pulling the trigger, let alone aim—when the enemy was on top of you and all you could hope to do was take out two or three who'd otherwise kill you.

The semi position could save you a dozen or so rounds, which, in a prolonged fight when ammunition was at a premium, might make the difference between life and death.

"Set up for extraction! Let's get out of here!" Lieutenant Hugele yelled over the radio as the Blues quickly moved into position. The gunships were hitting the far hillside with rockets and minigun or automatic machine-gun fire as the three Apache Troop lift ships began their short final approach.

Harding and Dockter were on the lead ship and opened up on the tree line as McIntosh readied for a bounce landing. The two following rescue helicopters kept their distance using McIntosh's lead, and within seconds the Blues were loaded aboard the helicopters and being lifted to a running start over the edge of the pickup zone.

The door gunners were still firing, and the hot shell casings were falling over the Blues in the open bays. Nobody complained. The NVA were in the clearing now, running out and firing at the lift ships that made a sharp banking turn to give the gunships room to strike. Within seconds, the helicopters were pulling away from the pickup zone, climbing away from the fight.

Throughout the tree line and clearings, enemy soldiers were scrambling to return fire or taking cover as the gunships made their runs, only to pop back out after they passed and fire blindly into the sky.

"My, my, my," Beal said in a quiet voice, studying the slowly diminishing pickup zone. "They're everywhere." He held on to his M16 and aimed it back toward the hillside without firing. Cortez and the Wise Guy covered the area as well, holding their fire too, knowing they were well beyond range. Still, their rifles and machine guns covered the hillside. Old habits were hard to break.

Nobody spoke. When the door gunners ceased fire, the helicopter bay was surprisingly quiet except for the comforting rotor noises of the lift ship.

They were out, and they were safe. Now the labored weariness would set in; the full weight of the long night's wait and day's activities and actions would press against their consciousness.

The Wise Guy grinned and shook his head, but even he was too tired to make a joke. The men of the point squad were covered in dirt, dried blood, and gunpowder. Their eyes were heavy, and their unshaven faces carried streaks of mud they hadn't had time to wipe off.

They had rescued two of the missing Rangers, pulled them out of the enemy's clutches, and Cortez had also managed to save the lives of two grunts in the process.

While there was real remorse at not having found the remaining two Rangers, there was some very real satisfaction at what they had accomplished.

Far across the countryside, the sun was beginning to fall over the dark and brooding rain forest. Riding off in the sunset seemed like a fitting tribute.

Barring any mechanical problems, antiaircraft machine-gun fire, or any other dangerous and yet all-too-often common occurrences in war, the business day for the Blues was over. It had been a successful mission by most standards, a good day for the way it made the rescuers feel about themselves and each other.

They'd gone into the trap and somehow, once again, managed to come out. Apache Troop was self-sufficient; it had its own lift ships, scouts, gunships, and quick-reaction platoon. Since the squadron had been formed, they had learned to rely on each other in ways many other units might not understand. The scouts flew at treetop level over the jungle just ahead of the Blues' ground forces to make sure they weren't walking into an ambush, while the gunships circled high above ready to assist, if needed.

The lift-ship crews lifted the Blues in and out of the jungle and served as medevacs when the Blues were wounded. It wasn't a hypothetical structure, just a real-world understanding of how things were. Each time one of the platoons had taken casualties, it was a combination of the other platoons that had come to their rescue. It was a symbiotic relationship in which each relied heavily on the other for its survival.

# CHAPTER TWENTY-EIGHT

Three thousand feet in the cool late-afternoon air, with Cambodia gradually disappearing behind them and the more familiar stretches of jungle directly below, the Blues began to relax.

While some slept upright in awkward sitting positions, leaning against rifles or equipment, others, like Specialist Cortez and the Wise Guy, were recounting the day's activities.

"A lot of bunkers," the Wise Guy said over the noise of the helicopter. The pitch of the blades changed sometimes, and the chopping sound would turn into a series of pops. "Had to be a company or more," he added.

Sergeant Ed Beal nodded in agreement. "At least a company," Beal said. "Did you see them scramble out after us when we were leaving?"

Cortez nodded, but something was clearly troubling him. "You think they're still down there? The Rangers, I mean?"

The Wise Guy shrugged. "I'd like to think so in one way, but hope to God they're not alive in another. Know what I mean?"

Cortez said he did. The thought of leaving behind wounded soldiers, especially people you had known personally, wasn't comforting. Leaving dead Americans was bad enough, and even that violated their personal code.

"If Cochrane hadn't laid down a base of fire when he

did, the whole team might've bought the farm. He saved their lives."

Cortez and Beal nodded in agreement.

"Jesus, I just wish we could've found them," Cortez said finally.

The Wise Guy looked at Sergeant Beal, who noticed the same thing, and then back at Cortez, who was preoccupied with the problem.

"Would you mind telling me what you were thinking when you decided to take on Ho Chi Minh's entire fucking army by yourself?" the Wise Guy asked, trying to draw Cortez out of his funk.

"I just wanted to help the wounded grunts. I don't know. Maybe I was thinking that somebody might do the same for me if I was stuck out there."

The Wise Guy shrugged again. "Depends," he said. "I mean, say, do you have a good-looking sister who might really be grateful to me for saving your ugly butt?"

Cortez's somber face turned questioningly to the smiling face of the wise-guy sergeant. What the fuck was he talking about now?

"I mean, *realllly* grateful?"

"Yeah," joined in Beal, "or how about rich parents. What's in it for us?"

In an instant, Cortez understood what the two were trying to do, and he laughed loudly, shaking his head and perhaps the troubling doubts that haunted him.

"Nothing!" he snorted. "Nothing at all!" They were his buddies, and he damn well knew they would be there for him if he needed it, just as he'd be there for them. It felt good seeing and knowing that they were covering him as he ran out to assist the wounded soldiers. Bloor, up on one knee, firing the machine gun at the enemy soldiers just as Beal, the Wise Guy, and the others had done. Their war was more than just mutual survival. It was people who had become family under harsh and brutal conditions, conditions that brought about bonds and friendships that were worth fighting for and saving.

"We don't have *S*'s on our chests, Pancho. We just do what we can. That's all," the Wise Guy added, thinking about something he had once heard the chaplain say about God not being able to be everywhere at once. Neither could Apache Troop. There were certain realities you came to understand firsthand and others that would come later. "We do what we can, and sometimes it just isn't enough," the Wise Guy said, more to himself than the others. Cochrane had been a friend of his as well. Being a combat realist didn't lessen the pain any or make the trip back any more comforting.

# CHAPTER TWENTY-NINE

After the Apache Troop lift-ship helicopters had touched down safely at Fire Support Base Buttons, the Blues slowly made their way back to their less than Spartan quarters. Behind them, the aircrews were securing the helicopters, tying down rotor blades, and then following the path the others had taken.

The walk was slow, and the men staggered. They were tired, and it showed. It was starting to rain again, a light, mist-like rain, so there wasn't the usual cloud of orange dust accompanying the landing. The soil was damp and stuck to the boots of the soldiers, revealing a lighter orange dust below. It was twilight. The sun had already gone down, but it was still light enough to see, although the shaded day was quickly giving way to a dark evening. Somewhere in the compound, a generator was droning on, while ribbons of electric light came filtering out of bunker openings.

A cat-size rat scurried to the top of a bunker near the flight line, studied the arriving Blues, and then indifferently shook off the mist and went about his business.

"Ah, there's no place like home," said the wise-guy sergeant. "Even if it is a hovel."

"What's a hovel?" one of the new replacements asked, a young private first class who couldn't have been more than

19 years of age, but since he was new he seemed a whole lot younger.

"It's like a shovel without the *S*. I guess it could be a hit too!" the Wise Guy replied. "Fortunately enough for us, the Army made it to dig ourselves out a miserable little dwelling, sandbag it, chase the rats and snakes out, and call it home. A place to rest our weary s's."

Someone laughed behind them. It was Burrows. "Weary s's? Huh?" he groaned.

The Wise Guy grinned and nodded. "You like it? It's part of my no-joke-is-low-enough-for-a-war-that-sucks policy. Just doing my part for the war effort and morale."

"You ever think about fighting the war quietly?" asked Burrows, setting up the Wise Guy who knew he was heading into another ambush. "Say, maybe with hand gestures?"

Burrows was in a surprisingly good mood, which didn't startle the Wise Guy and the others as much as make them wonder where he was leading.

"Okay, I'll bite," the Wise Guy said. "Hand gestures, huh?"

"Yeah," Burrows replied. "You could call it 'winning hearts and mimes'!" Burrows laughed while the Wise Guy just stared at him blankly.

"Talk about bad jokes . . ."

"Sure, but you'll use it again. I know you," said the staff sergeant. "Just remember where you heard it, hot dog."

Coming up behind them, Lieutenant Hugele wanted to get a word or two to his people before they managed to store their equipment and filter out to their cramped dwellings. "You guys did well out there today," he said, speaking with a sincerity the platoon hadn't heard before. Thresholds were being crossed every day, and the rescue mission had brought them through another one. "I'm proud of you guys."

"Shit, Lieutenant!" said the Wise Guy. "Keep that up and we'll ask for a raise. Either that or a split-level hovel!"

Hugele laughed along with him. "You people deserve better than you receive at times. Specialist Cortez," the officer said, turning toward the California infantryman, "I didn't see what you did out there, but I've heard about it from enough people who witnessed it. I don't know what the awards and decorations officer has planned, but I'm sure what happened today will not go unrewarded." Hugele turned toward Burrows, who nodded in understanding and then fixed his stare on the wise-guy sergeant and Sergeant Beal. They understood as well. The staff sergeant would collect the statements from the squad leaders, who would write them up and forward them up the chain of command for approval. The look from Burrows was enough to let them know their role in the program.

"No sweat," the Wise Guy said as Beal nodded in agreement. "We'll take care of it." Burrows and the lieutenant seemed satisfied with the response. Cortez was still trying to be humble but not having much luck at it. No one, it seemed, would let him. Although the quiet Californian would downplay his actions, many of those who had witnessed the act would not, for several reasons—most notably because in that war where there were few high points or reasons to feel good, Cortez had given them one. His selfless, heroic act had made them all feel as though they were the good guys because he was one of their own. It was one brief shining moment they would all point to later on with a sense of real satisfaction, a sense of accomplishment of the kind the rescue mission had provided them. The war would always have its detractors, those who'd point accusing fingers and say, "You shouldn't have been there!" But the Blues could point back to missions like this and answer, "Yeah, well, there's the way things are, and the way things should be." They didn't have the luxury of distance, let alone of making policy decisions. Caught up in the fighting, they had only to deal with their own personal conflicts, the primary being the morality of their actions. The rescue mission and Cortez's act gave them something they could turn to with pride.

"Good job. Now get some rest," the lieutenant said as he turned to leave. "You earned it."

Watching the lieutenant leave, the Wise Guy said, "Not a bad guy, I mean for an officer," loud enough for Hugele to hear.

Sergeant Beal laughed. "Yeah, a shame he had to ruin a potentially promising career by not becoming an enlisted man. A pity, actually. I think he believed that rumor in officer's candidate school about officers being able to piss lemonade!"

"You mean they can't?" the Wise Guy said. Hugele's laughter rippled across the compound.

"What about Burrows?" Beal asked the Wise Guy, who turned and smiled at the staff sergeant.

"I don't know," the Wise Guy said. Then, turning to the professional soldier, added, "Say? Have you ever thought about making the Army a career?"

"Fuck off, you smart-ass!"

"So, does that mean no?"

Those who had heard the exchange were laughing as they made their way to their quarters. They were in a good mood, and not even the rain would dampen it. Staff Sergeant Burrows and the Wise Guy were discussing other matters and reaching a comfortable accord, a truce of sorts. From across the flight line, the pilots were working their way to a makeshift officers' club, among them Bartlett and McIntosh. Several seemed to be retelling the events of the day with elaborate hand gestures and laughter while others appeared to be content listening to the tale.

"We smoked 'em!" a new pilot said. McIntosh shook his

head wondering if the dumbass knew what he was talking about.

"We did well," McIntosh said.

"Fucking right we did! We kicked ass!"

"No," the scout pilot said, correcting the younger pilot. "We did well, and what's more, we were lucky. Sometimes that's enough." McIntosh broke away from the others and headed toward the mess tent to check to see if his crew could still get something to eat. There would be enough time to celebrate later.

Art Dockter had helped Harding tie down their aircraft before gathering up his things and heading toward the aircrew's bunker area. All he wanted was a shower and maybe eight good hours of sleep. Sitting in the helicopter for well over 12 hours had left his back and legs cramped. Other than the brief time he had on the ground supporting the Blues with his machine gun when they found Andrus, he had spent most of the time in the helicopter.

He was cold, wet, and hungry. He'd take a shower, change into a dry Nomex flight suit, and then go over to the mess hall to get something to eat. In the helicopter, he kept a few C rations, along with a change of clothes, a dry cotton/nylon-mix poncho liner, and a plastic poncho from when he had decided to make the helicopter his temporary home. He also kept a few body bags to use as makeshift sleeping bags in bad weather. More than a few times an unsuspecting trooper was disturbed by the sight of the body bags shifting around in the bay of the helicopter. But it was the talking in the sleep that at times scared the crap out of the more superstitious.

The stored items were everything he needed, but it wasn't enough to discourage him from doing what he wanted to do. That is, until he saw the rats. The first one scurried from one bunker to the next without even pausing; the second took its time. Those two didn't necessarily dissuade Dockter. However, the next four were enough. Or maybe it was the jagged trail left by the snake as it followed the rush of rats to the first bunker. The only snakes that the tired door gunner could ever recall seeing in Vietnam were the deadly mud-brown cobras. "Common cobras," someone had said. "They're here because the rats eat the garbage we create; the snakes eat the rats. This isn't a base camp, it's a fucking environmental buffet!" The way the cobras reared up and spread their hoods was enough to make the sight a memorable frigging Kodak moment. The shower was a definite as was the change of clothes and the hot meal, but afterward, he'd head back to the Huey. The fighting part of the war was easy. It was trying to survive the daily routine that was getting to be the real problem.

# CHAPTER THIRTY

In the week that followed, there would be four additional search-and-rescue attempts for Cochrane and Laker, each yielding less than the first. Sniper fire and attacks against the search parties made finding the missing Rangers impossible. It didn't look good because within a week to 10 days, the American forces would be pulling out of Cambodia.

The first rescue attempt and the others that followed weren't the big story. The "invasion" was still front-page news. The focus was on the Cambodian incursion, and in the end, the credit for its success would slowly begin to filter down to those who designed and carried it out. In short, to those who deserved it.

But that would take years to sort out, and in some cases, decades. Official histories and after-action reports would point to agreed-upon references or facts citing those who completed the necessary paperwork and told their stories.

During the hectic 61 days of the operation, scores of congressional visitors, dignitaries, and overseers admired the mounds of captured weapons and equipment, looking over the booty while pondering its significance and making professional assessments.

Reporters and other news people reported what happened or colored their stories to fit their political or private agendas.

In fact, in the waning days of the invasion, just after an

attack on FSB David, a prominent news personality flew in to view the aftermath. Along with him came a number of REMFs. The acronym applied to all those soldiers not directly involved in the fighting; spelled out it means rear-echelon mother-fuckers. REMFs were usually clothed in crisp, clean uniforms and haughty demeanors and never did much for the soldiers in the field. The REMF major accompanying the VIP was disgusted by the helicopter crew, which, he was shocked to find, had, he thought, lost some of its military bearing. Combat area or not, REMFs felt soldiers and aircrew would damn well conform to military standards.

"Who's in charge here?" the major asked as Chief Warrant Officer Senkowski came around the helicopter and stopped just short of the major without saluting. An enemy AK-47 assault rifle with a folding stock was cradled on his left shoulder. Senkowski reached to keep the weapon from sliding, and the REMF officer caught himself starting to return a salute that wasn't coming and lowered his half-raised arm. Soldiers didn't salute in the field and especially in the forward combat areas. It was too dangerous.

"I am, sir," Senkowski said. "How can I help you?"

"You can help me, Mister, by finding some water and having you and your people shave. We have some very important people visiting here today."

"Excuse me, sir?"

"I said it might be a good idea to find some water and clean up. Have I made myself clear?"

Senkowski smiled. "Major, we've been living out of our helicopters for going on a week now. This . . ." he said, pointing to the helicopter's resting place, which lay outside of the fire support base's perimeter, to emphasize the point, "this is where we laager. If I knew where any water was, I'd drink it. What's more, I don't really give a rat's ass about your VIP. We're fighting a war. Now, you'll have to excuse me, Major, but I have to see if I can scrounge up some food for my people after we patch up a few bullet holes in the aircraft." And, with that rebuke, the veteran pilot went back to what he was working on while the REMF major stared in disbelief before wandering back to the safe confines of the fire support base.

"Keep that attitude, up, Mr. Senkowski, and you'll never make general," his door gunner said, while Senkowski laughed and went back to work. He didn't have stars in his eyes. Certainly not about the war, and certainly not about anything else lately. The war quickly made you a realist. At least when you were right in the middle of it and not viewing it from the sidelines where you could say, "Great show!", straighten your uniform, and fly away when it was convenient.

Forward combat elements played catch-as-catch-can. Even the everyday luxuries like showers, regular sleep, and meals didn't apply. The war always took priority. But even after Cambodia, when they returned to their bases of operation, there would still be the war. Living conditions would improve, but they still wouldn't come up to the standard enjoyed by those in the rear areas. For the Cav's LRRP/ Rangers, missions would continue, and perhaps because of what happened to one of their teams outside of Fire Support Base David, they'd be a little more cautious and, too, more aggressive toward the enemy. Vengeance through professionalism. They'd choose their ambushes carefully just as they had in the past, but there would be a harder edge to them now; the lessons learned wouldn't fall on deaf ears.

As for Apache Troop, they'd have their own lessons learned, as well, and of course, others' lessons learned to correct. The after-action reports sometimes altered events, courtesy of the writer making out the report. In one instance, the finding of "The City"—the huge enemy bunker complex with acre after acre of well-constructed and maintained fighting positions, storage facilities, and training areas—would be credited to Bravo Troop, 1st of the 9th, even though others contended it was discovered by Apache Troop scouts working the area.

Warrant Officers Bill McIntosh and Rick Pearce, two veteran Apache Troop scout pilots, had found the facility and had taken fire requesting assistance as they skirted the edge of the vast complex just six miles south of Snuol. McIntosh and Pearce called in their find as they pulled back to refuel. Scout helicopters from Bravo Troop took over, only to meet the same hostile fire as did McIntosh and Pearce. With reinforcements and a ground ready-reaction force on the way, the Bravo Troop birds were credited with the discovery. While it seemed a small point of contention to onlookers, the rivalry between the troops of the 1st of the 9th Cav—not to mention any other helicopter-borne unit—was a matter of principle as well as the stuff of legend.

The scouts, gunships, and Blues took their jobs seriously and, at times, zealously defended what was theirs, demanding their due. Respect of varying degrees was directly related to the credit received or denied for important actions.

Not long after the rescue mission, a group of pilots from Apache Troop was sitting in another unit's makeshift officers' club when someone from that unit made the error of toasting his own unit as having the best pilots in country. Stupid. Like the old adage about bringing a knife to a gunfight, or so a few Apache Troop pilots thought overhearing the boast. "Excuse me?" a veteran gunship pilot said in a mocking voice, looking up from his table of semi-shitfaced Apache Troop pilots. He obviously did not really believe what he and the others had just heard. "What did you say?"

"I just toasted the best pilots in country!" the rival lieutenant said, giving the mixed bag of Apache Troop officers a smirk. Macho takes many forms.

"Thanks. We appreciate the compliment," the Cobra

gunship pilot said before turning back to the others at the table. They were snickering.

"Oh yeah? And just who do you think you are?" The sarcasm in the lieutenant's voice was heavy and lingering.

"Apache Troop, the 1st of the 9th Cav. As you said, the best pilots in the war. Nice of you to say so. Damn nice!"

The lieutenant from the other unit shook his head. "I wasn't drinking to you. I was drinking to us," he said, gesturing to the rival unit's emblem behind the bar while making certain the table of visitors had seen that they were surrounded by the officers and pilots from his company.

"Ah! Then, point of contention," the Apache Troop gunship pilot said with a special smile at the lieutenant. Technically, the lieutenant outranked the warrant officer Cobra pilot, but the gunship pilot didn't really give a rat's ass.

"What?" the lieutenant asked, making the mistake of getting too close to the Apache Troop table and standing with his hands on his hips as he did; a defiant gesture at best. The challenge that wouldn't go unnoticed or unaccepted.

"It's a matter of social etiquette. Point of contention," repeated the Apache Troop Snake pilot, a little louder for the pleasure or attention of those seated at the table and for the rest of those in the club. "Here. Let me put it another way. Point of fucking contention. You, sir, are obviously unaware of the folly you speak. You haven't the barest idea of what you speak. But you will!" More than a little drunk, the Apache Troop gunship pilot was accepting the challenge while nodding to those at his own table who were enjoying the show.

"And what is that supposed to mean?" said the rival lieutenant. He was a little too cocky for the Snake pilot's liking, who only leaned back in his chair and let out an audible "Ooooooh."

"Whoa! Wait a minute! At ease. Calm the fuck down!" a scout pilot said, getting to his feet. "Everybody calm down! I'd better explain," he added, taking up where the gunship pilot had left off. "What he meant to say was that you and these other rear-area, crop-dusting motherfuckers are full of shit, but you're all too stupid to know it. Gentlemen. Cover me! I'm going in!" the Apache scout pilot said, then turned abruptly and, with his head down and neck braced, tackled the unsuspecting lieutenant with a drunken charge, wrestling him to the floor. Good clean fun! Sort of. Within seconds, the odd mix of warrant officers, lieutenants, and occasional captain from Apache Troop had the rival pilot stripped bare and retreating, as they pelted the man and the rest of his companions with half-filled or unopened cans of warm beer.

It was the barrage of cans that kept the rival officers at bay.

"As we all can see, Lieutenant, you don't have the balls to make that claim!" the scout yelled as he held up the officer's flight suit. "But we do!" Running short on ammunition and ready to break station, the Apache Troop pilots retreated out the door as the angry mob of rival pilots quickly followed.

Commandeering the first vehicle they could find—a deuce-and-a-half truck—the drunk and rowdy pilots drove it into the door frame of the O-club. Engine revved and ready, they waited as a lone scout pilot climbed above the club's entrance, positioned himself with a thumbs-up sign, and then pissed on those unfortunate few rival pilots who had squeezed out the door to continue the fight.

"You crazy bastards!" someone yelled from the inside of the officers' club as the Apache Troop pilots stripped two more would-be combatants bare and flung them back through the door while the scout pilot figured out how to button his fly and then jumped in the waiting truck. Treetop level always seemed better for the attack.

"Ah! Now you begin to understand why we're the best!

Audacity! Courage! And a fine sense of don't-give-a-shit! It's been a pleasure, but we gotta run!" The cry was still ringing in the victims' ears before the dust from the road had cleared.

Everyone knew the calm after the Cambodian raid wouldn't last and that Apache Troop would soon be back in the countryside spoiling for a fight. Perhaps no one appreciated that more than those in the rear areas who had to contend with them.

The O-club affray was a lesson in rivalry that earned Apache Troop a reputation for more than just combat skills, which was a good thing to those who relished the unit's sense of difference despite the fact that, at times, it concerned Army brass. "Well, screw 'em!" summed up one troop pilot. "We ain't in the Army anyway. We're in the Cav!" The war would continue for several years after the fall of 1970, and not all of the battles fought during those years would involve bullets and bombs. Some would begin and end with calculated laughter. For some of the pilots of Apache Troop, the rescue mission was the yin to their less-than-conventional Army yang. Any balance, they found somewhere in between.

# CHAPTER THIRTY-ONE

U.S. losses during the Cambodian raid averaged over 40 soldiers a day, and while the figure would never total more than those of the previous wars, one significant statistic would emerge. The significant and perhaps alarming statistic was that the likelihood of being crippled or maimed rose dramatically in Vietnam and Cambodia.

The numbers and documented medical cases revealed that there was a 300-percent greater chance than in World War II and a 70-percent greater chance than faced the soldiers in Korea.

The numbers also revealed that the 1st Cavalry Division, "the Cav," suffered the most losses of any Army division (5,444 killed in action and 26,592 wounded in action) while inflicting the most enemy losses. Leading those figures was the 1st of the 9th.

Early in the fighting, many of those wounded or killed came from the helicopter patrols. Later, the figures would expand to include the infantry who bore the responsibility of engaging the enemy in ground combat. It was their job to push into the bases and sanctuaries and drive out the enemy.

While the initial casualty figure for the North Vietnamese Army and Viet Cong was staggeringly high during the first few weeks of Operation BINH TAY because of the massive bombing, constant artillery attacks, and roving helicopter scout and gunship patrols, the numbers slowly began to decrease as the raid wore on.

The North Vietnamese Army and Viet Cong were once again adjusting to the situation and adapting to the tactics of the American offensive. With their bases and sanctuaries destroyed and the element of surprise denied them, the war turned back to the familiar North Vietnamese game of hide-and-seek.

With the vast stretches of rolling jungle and rain forests available to them, the Viet Cong and North Vietnamese Army retreated farther into the countryside, giving them the room they needed to lick their wounds without too much worry of detection. The raid had not caught him completely by surprise, and the enemy had had time to move some of his stores and provisions. The enemy's headquarters had given the word to evacuate the area, but the orders were slow to filter down to the units. When the push finally did occur, the retreating enemy was fighting as much to withdraw his equipment and weapons as he was to oppose the advancing Americans.

Millions of rounds of ammunition and more than 100,000 rocket and mortar rounds were captured when the Viet Cong and NVA bases were overrun. Thousands of tons of the latest equipment and explosives were captured along with it. One oddity came near the city of Snuol, Cambodia, where Lieutenant Colonel Thomas Fitzgerald kicked in the door to a weapons warehouse and, to his surprise and amazement, discovered hundreds of flintlock rifles. Accompanied by the Apache Troop Blues, Fitzgerald realized the enemy had been collecting and storing the multitude of weapons for some time. It also showed the level of NVA and Viet Cong control over the weapons in the vicinity—and over the local population.

However, while several thousand enemy soldiers were

killed in the initial drive, the majority of Viet Cong battalions and NVA divisions had scattered.

Over the millennia, the Vietnamese had become masters of avoiding large-scale confrontations, choosing instead to attack and withdraw when such actions proved advantageous and convenient. They learned to win by degrees, using patience and perseverance as tools. History and American B-52s had been exacting teachers, and what they learned recently was added to their carefully stored knowledge and immediately applied.

In the years of fighting the Americans, they had learned a great deal. For instance, they learned that the helicopter gunships seldom traveled in bad weather and could not be used effectively at night, so they'd move their soldiers and equipment under the cover of darkness. It was then, too, that they'd conduct their attacks.

They had also learned that by spreading out their forces over a large jungle battlefield, they could minimize their casualties from both fixed artillery and helicopter aerial artillery. Carpet bombing was deployed against known jungle bases, but it couldn't eliminate all of the NVA safe havens and infiltration routes.

The North Vietnamese Army and Viet Cong had learned to press the enemy toward sunset and hit him at his weakest or most tired moments prior to dawn. They also knew that two soldiers positioned correctly with RPG-7s, the deadly Soviet shoulder-fired, rocket-propelled grenade, could take out a lift of three helicopters seconds after they touched down to pick up a platoon of soldiers. The tactic had worked more than a few times, just as had the ambushes the NVA set in landing zones for the helicopters they knew would come. Placing .51-caliber antiaircraft machine guns at the most advantageous positions, they'd wait until the line of helicopters touched down before opening up. Like skilled boxers, they learned to feint and jab, to hit when and where they could before quickly moving away from the larger, more dangerous opponent. But this war wasn't a match for style or points. It was a fight of duration, and if they couldn't knock the opponent out, then they'd outlast him. Weak in the legs and reeling from the solid hits they were taking, the NVA nonetheless hung in there.

The NVA and VC became experts at their profession because they had paid dearly to gain that knowledge and skill. Everything had come at a price, and the costs were evident across the war-weary nation and in the homes of wailing wives and mothers.

When the forward fire support bases like David were shut down and the areas abandoned, the NVA would once again work to occupy the areas, each time less openly.

In the closing days of the invasion, the enemy began to apply his expertise to his strategy and was having a certain amount of success. But then, the timetable had been provided in advance by the politicians, and the NVA knew the exit routes from Cambodia. Nevertheless, their efforts would be small and disjointed.

To their credit, even with the NVA bases destroyed and much of their stores and ammunition captured, they had somehow avoided the large-scale defeat. That proved to be a point of frustration for those who planned the raid.

While the Americans and their allies were poised for the big battle, which never materialized, they had their hands busy with the smaller battles, which were springing up everywhere.

But if the enemy had learned from his opponent, so, too, had the Americans. With technology on their side and their own recently acquired expertise in jungle warfare, the Americans began to pick and jab away at the NVA and Viet Cong. They, too, would attack and withdraw at their convenience and at the most opportune time. Discretion was not only the better part of valor. Sometimes it just made damn good tactical sense. The fight was far from over, and it was well into the late rounds. There would be no clear-cut winner. No uncontested champion. Everything would be left to the decision.

# CHAPTER THIRTY-TWO

In the days and weeks that followed the Cambodian raid, the border regions of Tay Ninh and Binh Long provinces were notably quiet. Gone, for a while at least, were the distant rumblings, the muffled thumps and *whoomphs* of artillery rounds slamming into the target areas, and the ripping tears of random machine-gun fire. Gone, too, were the evening displays of Christmas-colored warfare—the white star clusters or parachute flares, the staggered, stitched red lines of tracer rounds from American and allied weapons meeting the enemy's green tracer rounds against the black velvet backdrop.

The days were equally uneventful. The war was taking a break, a hiatus that no one believed would last. Like weathermen caught in the eye of a hurricane, the veterans in Apache Troop knew the calm was only temporary; they savored it anyway.

Before the push into Cambodia, distant towns and villages such as Tay Ninh, Song Be, Quan Loi, and Loc Ninh were hit frequently by enemy mortars or rockets, and the wailing sirens of the incoming artillery early-warning system echoed across the provinces. Ground probes were commonplace, and periodic all-out assaults or attacks against fire support bases and base camps made them places of interest and topics for conversation, as well as places not to be. The sound of the NVA bugles signaling an attack was all too familiar to those who inhabited the bases. The bugles' cry meant the attacks were in earnest and for possession of the sites. For life and death. It was real-life capture the flag and king of the mountain, and any way it happened fell within the game plan. There were no rules. No time-outs.

Once an assault began against an outpost, the strategy of the enemy became simple. Break through the barbed wire, blow a hole or avenue of approach between the perimeter bunkers and fighting positions, and then swarm over the base, killing everyone in it. There was no time to take prisoners in a ground attack. It was kill or be killed, and everyone knew it.

Fire Support Bases Buttons, Ike, Jamie, Carolyn, Becky, and Grant were repeatedly hit by North Vietnamese Army assaults, some so hard at times that when the sun finally came up and the gun smoke from the weapons and choking black smoke of the fires caused by the explosives finally cleared, hundreds of enemy soldiers lay dead in the barbed wire, while the dead Americans littered the small jungle bases, and the wounded on both sides cried in anguish.

Even the American Army's base camps in Quan Loi and Tay Ninh became the constant focus for harassment fire and attack. Bits and pieces of destroyed aircraft attested to the accuracy of the enemy's attacks. The 25th Infantry Division base camp at Tay Ninh, which also housed units of the 1st Cav and the 11th Armored Cavalry Regiment, earned the nickname of Rocket City for its almost nightly barrage of enemy incoming rounds. The black, acrid smoke from direct hits on the aircraft in Quan Loi seemed part of the daily picture. Conversations about the nightly attacks took on an almost causal tone as a result.

"So where'd they hit you guys last night?"

"They missed the airfield, but they blew the shit out of the mess tent. Powdered fucking eggs everywhere."

It wasn't uncommon for grunts stationed at Tay Ninh to climb on the roofs of their hootches to watch the enemy 122mm rockets and 81mm mortars hit. It wasn't the safest seat in town, but it often provided cheap entertainment to those who had learned to come to terms with the attacks.

Following the 61-day raid, the frequency and impact of the enemy attacks were minimal, and the Red Alert (for imminent combat status) was downgraded to the cautionary Yellow Alert or even the all-clear Green Alert category. The roving helicopter scout-and-gunships patrols—the hunter-killer Pink Teams—turned into what some pilots called Sunday drives, and the infantry reconnaissance missions were strolls that accompanied them. The Blues referred to the missions as picnics, and the idea of the enemy in the area took on as much importance as would a handful of meandering wasps or marauding ants. They were there, and they were annoying, but they wouldn't spoil the outings. The nests and colonies were gone—or appeared to be.

With many of the veteran Blues already gone or preparing to leave, Burrows used the downtime to train his new people, working the new replacements into the shape he knew they needed, even if they sometimes didn't want to believe it themselves. Just because they couldn't pick a fight with the enemy those days didn't mean the NVA weren't biding their time. Burrows had been a professional combat soldier long enough to know the lull was only temporary. The raid didn't wipe the enemy out, let alone his resolve to keep fighting to win. Instead, it only set his timetable back. In the tug-of-war fighting that was Vietnam, pulling the opponent three steps closer to the finish line didn't guarantee victory. It just meant you had the momentum on your side.

As a result of the raid, the Viet Cong and NVA lost the equivalent of three regiments, over 11,000 soldiers, and they'd have the long and arduous job of rebuilding their military strength, not to mention resupplying their stores and ammunition. But they were a patient people. Having to rebuild their strength wouldn't stop them from striking back. Harassment fire and catching their opponents off guard had been the foundation of their overall battle plan for centuries. Any quiet time would be short-lived.

Prior to the push into Cambodia, Apache Troop was in the process of moving from Tay Ninh to Song Be by way of Phuoc Vinh. By design, the shift in responsibilities and area of operations would change the complexion of the regional strategy once again with the Cav in the lead.

By the end of June, the move had been completed, and the troop was busy moving from the underground bunkers and rat hole sleeping areas into newly constructed hootches. Thanks to First Sergeant Joseph Sparacino, the new hootches were clean, dry, and relatively rat free, which for Fire Support Base Buttons was saying something. If all wasn't right with the world, then at least in the border regions things were considerably better. The quiet time allowed for additional training, and Staff Sergeant Burrows was taking advantage of it.

"The secret of busting an enemy ambush is to assault the ambush," Burrows explained to a group of Blues sitting around the platoon's command post. "While two or three will try to pin you down, the others will rush to outflank or maneuver around you."

Some of the new replacements weren't looking like they were buying it. To them, charging machine-gun fire didn't seem like a safe or even smart way of surviving, so the burly staff sergeant tried to clarify his position.

"You have to break through the ambush, overrunning the enemy straight on, otherwise he'll pin you down and pick you apart in a kill zone. In fact, a few months ago, we had an NVA company . . ."

While the new replacements were caught up in the

training and war story, the veterans in the platoon were discussing more pertinent matters; the seeming lack of interest and attention annoyed Burrows.

"So this lady I met in a bar in Sydney had flavored nipples!" explained a spec four from Burrows' squad.

"Get outta here!" the Wise Guy said while everyone in the point squad laughed or chuckled.

"Swear to God!" the spec four added, holding his hand over his heart as the Wise Guy, Beal, and Cortez listened with keen interest. "She put candy flavoring or something on them."

"What flavor?"

"Grape. I'm talking *real* taste treats."

"Did you use a condom for your tongue?" the Wise Guy asked. The second round of laughter caught Burrows' attention and ire.

"You have something to add?" the staff sergeant bellowed across the small, canvas-walled room.

The Wise Guy grinned. "We were just discussing the importance of good oral hygiene," he said. "And maybe keeping abreast of world affairs, too, so to speak."

"I'd appreciate everyone's attention since we have a mission at first light, and some of the new people don't have the benefit of experience."

The Wise Guy nodded. "Some of us don't have all of the experience we'd like to either!"

"Good oral hygiene?" Cortez whispered.

The Wise Guy shrugged. "It was all I could think of at the time."

The following day's mission at first light was uneventful. Three hours into it, the patrol hadn't produced anything of consequence. If the NVA were in the area then they were doing a damn good job of hiding. The bunker complex the platoon had been sent to search showed no signs of recent use.

Cooking pits in the dugout kitchens were carboned and cold. The orange-clay trails beneath the jungle canopy were wind-worn and weathered, leaving the spoor—the sandal and boot prints or markings the enemy made in passing—almost indistinguishable to the practiced eye.

"Ancient history. Nobody's home," Sergeant Beal whispered to the Wise Guy as they studied the old trail.

The sounds of the surrounding jungle also told the two veteran point men everything they needed to know about the bunker complex. The birds, lizards, and monkeys were emitting screeching cries, piercing whoops, or low, guttural grunts or croaks.

While the noise might have unnerved a few of the new arrivals, it brought a sigh of relief from the two veterans. They knew that the birds and animals could sense the carnage in approaching combat and shied away for survival. Mating calls and gunfire didn't go hand in hand, something both Beal and the Wise Guy well understood. The symphony of the rain forest was well received.

"Music to the ears, partner, and this is a jungle concert!" the Wise Guy said, surveying the empty bunker complex. "Like Tarzan said to Jane. Nobody here to spear our butts. Life's good!"

Beal nodded just as the point squad's radioman handed the squad leader the radio handset. "Blue's on the horn for you."

"Alpha Four Four. Go," Beal said into the handset. He listened intently, rogered Lieutenant Hugele's transmission, then returned the handset to the RTO. "Saddle up!" he said to the rest of the point squad as the Wise Guy asked what was up. The mission was only half over, and even though the bunker complex was empty, the platoon still had a trail it could work.

"I don't know. Blue wants us back at the landing zone in

pickup posture. The choppers are on their way to pick us up."

The extraction of the four squads would take three lift formations, the squad leaders standing, holding their rifles over their heads, guiding the helicopters in as the rest of the platoon faced outward, awaiting the pickup while covering the tree line. Divided into three groups and split again into left- and right-loading patterns, the Blues knelt in the knee-high grass and covered the walls of the surrounding jungle from the open pickup zone.

Within minutes, the choppers could be heard *whopping* their way over the trees, the clumsy-looking, round-nosed Hueys quickly setting down as the Blues hurried aboard. Eight seconds was the buffer. That's all they would wait. Time enough for everyone to get on board before the lift ships lowered their noses then pulled pitch in their familiar running start. On Charlie Alphas—combat assaults—the Blues would straddle the helicopter skids, and, as the Hueys touched down, the platoon would jump off and fan out on the landing zone, prone. In the cold LZs—the quiet landing zones—the Blues would wait for the lieutenant's command to move out. However, in the hot LZs—those that the enemy occupied—the Blues would charge into the tree line returning fire. The lift ships only touched down for eight seconds on the insertions, too. Their goal was to get airborne as quickly as possible, while it was the platoon's job to rout out the enemy.

As the Hueys lifted out of the pickup zone, the door gunners fired a volley into the wall of jungle. If the NVA or Viet Cong were hiding in the underbrush, the machine-gun rounds would keep their heads down. Safely aboard the helicopters, the platoon would get comfortable for the ride to where they were going. Time to sleep or think or talk about everything in general or something in particular.

"Uncle Ho's neighborhood . . ." the Wise Guy said, surveying the rain forest below.

"You know Ho Chi Minh wasn't his real name," Burrows said, causing the young buck sergeant to turn back in interest.

"What?"

"I said Ho Chi Minh wasn't his real name. That's just one of the ones he used."

"So what was it? Chuck Chi Minh? Bob maybe?"

The staff sergeant looked at the Wise Guy, wondering why he even bothered, but he decided to keep trying anyway. The kid had potential in spite of himself.

"His real name was Nguyen Sinh Cung, which he changed to Van Ba, then to Nguyen Ai Quoc, and when he visited in Brooklyn he used Nguyen Tat Thanh . . ."

"Whoa!" said the Wise Guy, having trouble with what Burrows was saying. "Brooklyn? As in Brooklyn, New York?"

Burrows nodded. "For a year or so in the 1920s, before he moved to Paris, which was years before he changed his name to Ho Chi Minh, which just means 'He who enlightens.' "

"No shit?"

"No shit."

The Wise Guy mulled it over a bit before replying. "Maybe that's where he got the idea for the revolution, because of all the gangsters and machine guns. Just think! Had he moved to Hollywood instead, Khe Sanh would've been a fucking musical! Say, you ever think about teaching history?"

"That and geography. Most Americans can't even find Vietnam on the map, let alone tell you anything about it!"

"Easy," said the Wise Guy. "Go to the Philippines and take a left. It's Iowa I have trouble finding . . ."

"Sure. You're here. You have more than a vested interest.

The trouble to most people, it's just some distant place they see each night on their TVs, like 'Gilligan's Island'—it's someplace tropical, only they can't exactly tell you where. They can't tell you the first thing about Cambodia or Vietnam, but they're sure what we're doing is wrong and that what we're doing here is a crime. The crime is, they don't know anything about the people, their struggles, let alone the ethnic problems."

" 'Gilligan's Island,' huh?" The Wise Guy laughed. "That should've been my line."

"I thought you'd appreciate it."

"Ah, the when-in-Rome approach?"

"There, too. Anyway, back home, we're on everyone's shit list as a result."

"So whose shit list are we on now that we have to make two combat assaults in one day?" the Wise Guy asked, pulling Burrows out of his thoughts.

"Nobody's!" said the acting platoon sergeant, looking somewhat perplexed. "We're not going on another combat assault. We're going to a USO show!"

"What?" chimed in Cortez, who had his eyes closed but found a reason to open them. A few of the other members of the point squad who had heard what Burrows had said leaned closer as well.

"I thought you guys knew," Burrows explained. "We're going back to Buttons. They have some cheerleaders, dancers, or something, to entertain us."

"Cheerleaders?" Cortez asked, smiling.

"Dancers, mostly, but they achieve the same result," said Burrows.

"Aw right!" someone yelled while the helicopter bay filled with excited laughter.

"I wonder if they're from Australia?" the Wise Guy said, while the acting platoon sergeant wondered what that had to do with anything. Not that he'd get an answer, because the young buck sergeant was lost in his own thoughts, thoughts that had a lot to do with grape.

# CHAPTER THIRTY-THREE

A hastily erected stage had been constructed near the main runway at Fire Support Base Buttons. Festive red-white-and-blue banners carrying the USO logo adorned a small platform to which someone had added a microphone and public address system. A sign behind the stage read: THE USO SALUTES THE FIRST CAV!

By the time the Blues touched down and stored their weapons and equipment, much of the space near the small stage had been taken by GIs who restlessly formed a U-shaped audience, waiting for the show to begin. Most sat before the stage, but others elected to stand and watch. They'd heard song and dances before; the Wise Guy heard one soldier say, "The last time I seen a song and dance like this, I was at the recruiting station sitting up close and taking it in. I think I'll stand back this time."

An Army public relations officer introduced a list of dignitaries who were acknowledged with polite applause, mostly from the other assembled officers. The warrant officers and enlisted men were there for something else. As the PRO introduced the four women who made up the traveling show, they bounded on the stage with practiced strides while the whoops and hollering of the soldiers drowned out much of the noise from the still-operating flight line.

According to the master of ceremonies, the four young lovely ladies, who were clad in short skirts, tight blouses,

and white go-go boots, had their share of entertainment
credentials, among them engagements in Las Vegas and
various appearances on television specials. Not that it mattered to the GIs, who stared at the long-haired, long-legged,
well-built, smiling women, seeing all the credentials and
prerequisites they required. After a year in country on a forward fire support base, they didn't need to be told what
special talents the ladies had to offer. Their imaginations
supplied everything they needed to know—and more.

The show girls were doing their best to look at ease. The
GIs were doing their damnedest to look suave, and those
who had managed to clean up a little and comb their hair
had the advantage over those who were dust-covered, smiling dumbly, and scratching or holding their crotches.

"God, I hope they don't sing the 'Ballad of the Green
Berets,' " the Wise Guy said as the point squad looked for
places to sit. "I hate that fucking song."

"So do the Green Berets," said Burrows. "At least the
ones I know."

"Think they'll roller-skate nude? The dancers, I mean?"

Burrows looked at the Wise Guy, laughed, and shook his
head. "Don't count on it, hotshot. More than likely it'll be
some songs somebody somewhere thinks will be acceptable
and in good taste. 'Born Free,' 'The Sound of Music,'
or . . ."

"Country Joe and the Fish—'One, Two, Three. What Are
We Fighting For'?" said the Wise Guy.

"Not hardly. Besides, that whiny guitar crap isn't music
anyway."

"That's right," countered the Wise Guy. "You only like
that music where fat ladies sing with steel bras while hitting
notes that send dogs running."

"Up yours! That's culture."

" 'Stuck in ol' Lodi again', that's Creedence Clearwater
Revival!"

The music wouldn't be live, but the dancers would, and while an enlisted man worked at setting up the prerecorded program the entertainers would lip synch to, the ladies smiled and waved to the assembled soldiers. "Hi! Where you from?" one asked a GI up front while the others did much the same.

After a few false starts while trying to locate the beginning of the show on the tape, and harmonized voices and a full orchestra echoed over the PA system in brief snippets, the performers were ready to begin. With a finger-snapping one, and a two, and a turn of the ON switch to the tape recorder, the four entertainers broke into a well-rehearsed and choreographed stage act in sequence to a taped rendition of "Born Free."

By the time the lead vocalist was into the third verse, the show was interrupted by a scout helicopter high above the stage that was doing a little show of its own. The Loach, a small olive-drab OH-6 observation helicopter, hovered momentarily, attracting everyone's attention before roaring down the runway and quickly gaining altitude. Climbing vertically, pushing the helicopter to its limits, the pilot was attempting a maneuver that just by its name made it an impossible stunt.

"Jesus, he's doing a wingover!" Cortez said, holding one hand over his eyes to keep the sun's glare from obscuring his vision. Helicopters don't have wings, and the high, arcing loop the pilot was putting his through was something the manufacturer didn't recommend. Everyone, including the entertainers, had turned their attention to the sky as the helicopter began arcing over in a loop. The stunt was a practical impossibility, but the pilot carried it off.

But that was only half of the show. The difficult part came rushing home as the helicopter was rifling toward the ground at an accelerated rate of speed. If the pilot was going to pull it off, then he only had a few seconds to do it.

The tape-recorded show was still going on even though the entertainers had given up the act and were watching the falling helicopter.

"The fucker's crazy!" somebody said as GIs rapidly began to move away.

"Ain't he though!" the Wise Guy said while others in the Blues point squad agreed.

"A certified basket case." Cortez chuckled just as the pilot leveled it off and roared back down the runway only 20 or so feet above the ground, the yellow triangle of Apache Troop evident on the bulb nose of the aircraft. "Figures, he's one of ours."

The applause was spontaneous, and even the entertainers joined in as the angered and worried brass seemed less enthusiastic about the aerial acrobatics and flight demonstration. Somebody's heels would be locked somewhere soon, and somebody's butt would be fitted for dentures. It could've been Lou Rochet, the latest wildman to fly scouts, or any of the other hotshot Apache Troop pilots who had the balls to pull it off, and who'd respond "yes sir" or "no sir" in the appropriate places as he was being chewed out and then walk away from the butt-chewing with a smile anyway.

"He's in deep shit, right?" the Wise Guy asked.

Burrows nodded. "Deep shit."

"Good for him!" yelled the Wise Guy, jumping to his feet wildly, applauding and joining in with the rest of the Blues who were laughing and cheering as well. Burrows was applauding along with them.

The standing ovation was unusually loud and growing in intensity. The soldiers were applauding for reasons maybe only they best understood or appreciated.

First Sergeant Sparacino was trying hard to look upset. Slowly shaking his head, he tried to look disgusted, too, only he smiled in spite of himself. My people, he thought to himself. Balls the size of grapefruits, and the trouble is they know it!

# CHAPTER THIRTY-FOUR

"Hi!" said the blonde USO dancer to the Wise Guy from the edge of the deserted stage. "Where are you from?"

The show had been over for hours, and no one had expected the entertainers to return, not even the Wise Guy, who couldn't really explain why he was there, let alone come up with a good reason for hanging around the stage as long as he had before she came back.

"Huh?"

The shapely woman in her early 20s laughed, but the Wise Guy knew it was in fun, hardly demeaning. "I asked where you're from."

"Oh, Apache Troop," replied the Wise Guy.

The young woman laughed again as a thin, delicate hand brushed away a trail of golden locks from two glistening pools of sea-green eyes. "No. I mean, back home. You know, back in the World?"

"At times this place seems like the only world I know. Does it matter?" asked the Wise Guy, smiling.

"No, I guess not," the dancer replied, suddenly quiet.

"Seattle."

"Oh, Washington! I hear it rains a lot up there?"

The Wise Guy nodded. "A colder monsoon, maybe," he said.

"Well, did you like the show?"

The Wise Guy's grin widened. "You bet! What's not to

like? God! You're beautiful," he said, embarrassing the woman and himself in the process. Her cheeks were slowly turning red.

"Thank you. But I think you're just saying that because you haven't been with a woman in a while. Back home, you'd probably think I'm quite ordinary."

The Wise Guy shook his head, adamant in his response. "No," he said. "Even back in Seattle, someone would have to be blind or stupid not to notice you."

The dancer's green eyes held the Wise Guy's momentary gaze, and he was sure that something in the pools had warmed, something turned beneath the surface. "Thank you," she said, genuinely touched.

"This may sound stupid, but can I kiss you? I know it's asking a lot, but I'd just really like to kiss you."

"I don't know," the dancer said in a less than convincing tone.

"Please," he begged. "Just one kiss?" he said, already certain of her answer.

The young woman smiled and shrugged. Round bare shoulders rose and fell in a graceful move. "Sure! Why not?" When they embraced, the kiss wasn't long but it was surprisingly tender, and when it was over she still held him close. Her slender hands braced his lower back. Her right thigh pushed against his, sending a message to his heart and his head. His groin wasn't far behind in interpreting it either. "That was nice," she said, smiling again as the Wise Guy nodded.

"Maybe one more request?" he asked.

"What is it now?" To him her laughter sounded like music.

"Can we do it?" he said matter-of-factly.

"Excuse me?" she said, her laughter stopping as suddenly as it began. Still, she held him in her arms, studying him intently.

"I said, can we do it? You know, sleep together? Make love? Screw our brains out?"

"I don't know . . ." she said, shaking her head but still maintaining her embrace.

"Please?"

"Oh . . . sure," she said finally. "Why not? You seem nice."

Pulling the young sergeant forward, she gently led him down to the stage. With one hand, she pulled off the costume halter top as the Wise Guy stared at purple nipples perched atop small but well-shaped breasts.

"Here?" he said, quickly looking around.

"Why not? This is the place for a show." She laughed, drawing his head to her breasts as the stage suddenly dropped five or so feet in an air pocket.

Her breasts were surprisingly hard and didn't taste like grapes at all, more like dust as the second air pocket slammed the helicopter to the left, jerking the Wise Guy out of his dream. All around the open bay of the helicopter, the Blues in the point squad were trying to catch a few quick minutes of sleep on their way in after another mission. They were bone-weary from the patrol in the hot Vietnamese jungle, and at 2,500 feet, the temperature was several degrees cooler than it was on the ground, but still it wrapped around them like a comfortable blanket.

"What in the hell were you dreaming?" Staff Sergeant Burrows asked, staring at the Wise Guy.

"Why?"

"You were licking Bloor's helmet!"

"Sorry," the Wise Guy said, looking around as though he were trying to find a trail back into the dream. "Iron deficiency," he said finally.

Burrows shook his head, laughing as he took off his helmet and handed it to the buck sergeant. "Here you go, hotshot. You seem to need it more than I do. Try not to become anemic."

Placing the steel pot on the stock of his rifle, the Wise Guy leaned against it and smiled. His eyes were closed. "I'll settle not to become emotionally involved," he snorted. "But these days I'll take what I can get!" He was humming "Born Free."

# . . . AND FINALLY

There would always be those who'd second-guess the LRRP/Ranger team leader's decision to move the team after calling in their night-halt position, critics who'd wonder why he decided to move.

After all, standard operating procedure was to stay in place after fixing the team's location for the evening. SOP is fine in theory. In real life, there are many possible and plausible explanations—the team needed better cover and concealment to hide from the enemy while conducting its intelligence mission; it might have lost radio communications because of the weather or terrain (the PRC-25, the shoulder-carried radio, which was the team's main communication system, wasn't state of the art); the dense fog and heavy rain that plagued the rescuers could very easily have convinced the team leader to relocate the team. If the team couldn't establish a radio link to the outside world, then the dangerous world it found itself in could quickly have swallowed it up. Staff Sergeant Deverton Cochrane could have based his decision on any of a hundred valid reasons.

Judging from the large number of enemy positions in the immediate area, along with the signs of enemy activity in the region, it probably wouldn't have mattered if the team had remained in place for the evening. The LRRPs' discovery was inevitable. The NVA were encamped in force around them, and how they had managed to maneuver undetected through the area was a credit to the team itself. The job of the LRRP was never easy, all too often moving in a world of inches to live and seconds to die.

Praise should be given to Cochrane, too, because in the first few deadly minutes of the bitter firefight, he provided covering fire for the others, permitting their escape. Severely wounded and perhaps realizing there was no way for himself to survive, Cochrane motioned the rest of the team back as he held the enemy up, exchanging fire with NVA who were less than a few feet away. In the open kill zone there was no place to hide, so he fought a point-blank firefight with the enemy until it was over, the outcome inevitable. Ironically, Staff Sergeant Cochrane was named after a relative, Deverton Carpenter, a fighter pilot in the Pacific during World War II, who is listed as missing in action.

Recognition and credit must also be given to LRRP/ Rangers Ron Andrus, Royce Clark, and Dwight Hancock for their incredible actions. Surviving unbelievable odds is the result of more than just a reaction to fear, and how one survives the ordeal is more than mere instinct or training. It is a matter of character, the likes of which defined the Cav's Rangers and those LRRPs as well.

Finally, there were the volunteers from Apache Troop who literally risked it all to pull the missing Rangers from the closing grip of the North Vietnamese Army.

It's too easy to find cynics or critics who'll say the rescue mission was no big deal, let alone a major battle. Or to find those who'll point out how it could've best been prevented or better handled. But then, those kinds of cynics and critics seldom have heroes because they seldom face the firing lines.

Me? I'll take the ones I knew and served with in Vietnam and Cambodia. At a time when it seemed as though there was little to feel good about, I knew a few people who gave me something to believe in and something to be proud of, people who taught me that sooner or later we have a necessary battle in our lives, one that, in good conscience, we can't turn away from. That's when the test of our convictions and strength of spirit will take over. Whether we succeed is not really the issue; it's how we face the battle and how we can justify our actions afterward.

It was a lesson not easily learned, but one taught by more than a few good people. Even if I was a wise-guy sergeant, I was smart enough to learn that much.

This is my way of applauding.

# EPILOGUE AND AUTHOR'S NOTE

---

*Destiny is not a matter of chance; it is a matter of choice. It is not something to be waited for; it is something to be achieved.*

—William Jennings Bryan

I like Bryan's quote because it reminds us we need to get off our butts if we're ever to be what we want to be. It's not settling, but taking an active role in determining our own course of action for the routes we take.

On the downside, there are always prices to be paid for those choices and achievements.

Those LRRP/Rangers and members of Apache Troop best lived Bryan's quote. And they paid dearly. But they did it on their terms with pride and honor. Although it's sometimes easy to belittle the notion of honor—let alone any sense of accomplishment—for the sacrifices and efforts of that war, those men are to be applauded.

On October 7, 1992, First Sergeant Francis Anthony Cortez of Bravo Company, 2d of the 27th Infantry, 7th Infantry Division, was honored at Fort Ord, California, for his part in the rescue mission 22 years earlier.

Major General Marvin Covault, commander of Fort Ord, presented First Sergeant Cortez the Silver Star for gallantry for saving the lives of the two wounded soldiers while on the LRRP/Ranger rescue mission.

Before his family, friends and fellow 7th Infantry Division soldiers, Cortez explained, "I didn't even think about the danger I was in. I just knew that they weren't going to make it unless I did something. They needed help."

It was nobility of action, gallantry for which the Silver Star is awarded. The Silver Star is the nation's third-highest award for heroism in combat. However, its real value is more than the medal itself. At first glance, the gold decoration that's attached to the red-white-and-blue ribbon doesn't seem all that impressive.

In fact, the silver star from which the medal derives its name is embedded on the front of the award. It's so small that it seems like an afterthought. But the legend on the medallion's reverse restores the award's full measure of dignity with the inscription FOR GALLANTRY IN ACTION.

Gallantry is old-fashioned heroism, something the dictionary defines as a nobility of spirit, the kind that goes along with honor and duty at a significant cost.

Part of Cortez's cost was the 22-year delay in receiving the award and the recognition that went with it. Six years ago, when I had learned that he hadn't received the award, I began to track down eyewitnesses and collect statements from those who also took part in the mission.

Many of those contacted were as surprised as I had been and offered their statements and support. Others offered the help it takes to correct something like this. They knew that Cortez's heroic act deserved to be recognized because, on an otherwise dismal day, he showed the spirit we had all fought for. For us, the war wasn't about politics; it was about people.

Specialist Four Francis Anthony Cortez was recommended for a Silver Star for what he did in Cambodia during the rescue of the missing Rangers. His actions could easily have cost him his life. Caught out in the open and crying for help, the wounded soldiers' pleas stood out across the battlefield between machine-gun bursts.

It was Cortez alone who decided to help them. Placing his weapon down, he charged out to rescue the two—old-fashioned heroism with nobility of spirit.

Four statements were submitted by those who witnessed the incident, among them the troop commander, William D. Harris, who in his official statement said, "Specialist Fourth Class Francis A. Cortez distinguished himself by gallantry in action while engaged in military operations involving conflict with an armed hostile force ... Cortez was involved in a rescue mission of five soldiers from H Company, 75th Ranger Regiment, missing in action in Cambodia. While the unit was attempting to extract two of the five missing soldiers, they came under massive small-arms fire from an estimated company of North Vietnamese Army soldiers. A quick-reaction rescue force ... came in to reinforce and immediately encountered heavy enemy fire from a tree line across the field. Two soldiers in the QRF, the infantry quick-reaction force, were wounded and lay on the ground in range of the enemy fire. Specialist Four Cortez rose from his covered position and sprinted across an open field, under intense enemy small-arms fire, to the wounded soldiers. With complete disregard for his own safety, he extracted the two wounded soldiers, one at a time, to his covered position while taking fire from the enemy force in the tree line ... Cortez's actions were in keeping with the highest traditions of the military service and reflect great credit upon himself, his unit, and the United States Army." Impressive words describing an impressive act.

Ironically, the paperwork for Cortez's award was lost, which, considering the circumstances, was not unusual. The 1st Cavalry Division's area of operations was over 3,000 square miles, and Apache Troop worked in advance of the squadron and division headquarters. During the Cambodian operation, Apache Troop operated for more than half the length of the operation from a forward fire support base, living out of helicopters and bumming places to shower, eat, and sleep. Everything was temporary or borrowed. The troop simply made do. Meanwhile, their unit and orderly room was being shifted from Tay Ninh to a temporary home in Phuoc Vinh on their way to a more permanent site in Song Be. Considering that, and recalling the fact that tours of duty for soldiers in Vietnam were staggered so members of the troop were constantly transferring in and out of the country, it isn't surprising that the paperwork for the award was misplaced.

Believing that the Army would eventually take care of the matter, Cortez was not one to blow his own horn. He left Vietnam in August 1970. If Napoleon was right when he said an army moves on its stomach, then he forgot to mention that it occasionally has a nasty habit of sitting on its butt until someone gives it a boot, which is what Sergeant Robert "Ed" Beal and I did years later when we learned the matter of the award had been forgotten. As two squad leaders, we originally submitted the paperwork for the award to Staff Sergeant Burrows. However, more immediate concerns took priority, and we left believing our roles in the process were completed.

Diagnosed with malaria, Sergeant Beal was medevacked from Vietnam to Japan shortly afterward. I completed my tour of duty and rotated Stateside to a new duty assignment in September.

Staff Sergeant Robert Payton Burrows suffered a seemingly slight head wound in a small, no-name battle on October 14, 1970, and was medevacked to Long Binh after he became dizzy and disoriented. In the rear-area field hospital, the extent of his wounds became more apparent. A piece of shrapnel from an explosion had entered the staff sergeant's brain. Robert Payton Burrows died on the operating table. The platoon was in shock, but the war continued.

In the mid-1980s when the award's oversight was brought to the Army's attention by Cortez's former squad leaders, Ed Beal and I tracked down the original eyewitnesses across the United States and collected their statements, including documentation from the former platoon leader, troop commander, and squadron commander. The evidence was submitted to the awards and decorations branch of the Army staff, which after considerable review chose to deny the request.

No one who took part in the rescue mission denied that the incident had occurred or that Cortez deserved the award. According to the awards and decorations branch of the Army, the official clock had run out for combat awards for Vietnam. They said the award no longer fell within their jurisdiction, and they referred it to another military office for consideration, which promptly approved.

The 22-year delay didn't delete the impact on those who were present at the award ceremony. What shone through are the words of those who witnessed the event and of those, like Jerry Boyle and the Wise Guy, who were also on hand for Cortez's ceremony 22 years later.

Among the statements and evidence collected were the words from retired Army colonel Clark A. Burnett, the former squadron commander of the 1st of the 9th, who had this to say: ". . . Cortez did exhibit extraordinary heroism in rescuing wounded comrades. . . . I highly recommend that the Army duly recognize Cortez for his heroic actions in combat during the Cambodian operation. Time does not degrade his actions, nor should it." Colonel Burnett's comments did not go unheeded.

Warrant Officers Bill McIntosh and John Bartlett received awards for heroism during later operations in the war for doing what they normally did. In fact, an Army general who witnessed one of Bartlett's later actions awarded the Montana resident a Silver Star after one particularly dangerous mission.

Bartlett explained that "anytime anyone asks me about how I received my Silver Star, I tell them about the time in Cambodia when I didn't, and about Tony Cortez who earned it twice over." John Bartlett was one of the officers and eyewitnesses who provided a statement on behalf of Cortez, just as did former Army captain Jack Hugele (Blue), Ranger Ron Andrus, Ed Beal, and Duane Bloor. Each chose to praise Cortez while playing down his own efforts.

It is ironic that not one person in Apache Troop who took part in the rescue mission ever received any award or recognition for it in Vietnam, which is one of the primary reasons I wrote this book. It's a collective award and one I hope they wear with pride.

While many left the Army after Vietnam, First Sergeant Francis Anthony (Tony) Cortez chose to make the Army a career. He has served with Airborne, Ranger, and Special Forces assignments, taking part in numerous other conflicts around the globe.

Captain Keith Hauk, Cortez's former company commander at Ford Ord, was among the first to congratulate him on the award. "Even in his mid-40s he runs circles around us," said Hauk. "The soldiers of Bravo Company look up to him, and so do I. He's a professional's professional, and I'm glad to have him as my first sergeant."

And don't miss Kregg P. J. Jorgenson's
harrowing account of life and death as
a point man in Vietnam:

# ACCEPTABLE LOSS
## AN INFANTRY SOLDIER'S PERSPECTIVE

By Kregg P. J. Jorgenson

Published by Ivy Books.
Available in your local bookstore.

For a glimpse of this riveting book,
please read on....

For every soldier in Vietnam who was actually fighting in the field, there were five support personnel in large, reasonably comfortable, rear-area bases or camps to service them. Besides the infantrymen there were the military police, medical specialists, supply and transportation soldiers, administration personnel, communication, intelligence, laundry, and maintenance units, along with various other companies or detachments who the infantry or grunts referred to less lovingly as REMFs.

This acronym, said with a certain amount of disdain, meant that these people were rear-echelon motherfuckers. How close you were to the actual fighting and what you did whenever it began set the REMF boundary. Combat medics were okay, as were some artillery people, tankers, various pilots and crew, and certain other select personnel. Any and everyone else who didn't fall into those classifications were REMFs and despised and maybe secretly envied because of their safe jobs.

"You see, it has to do with war stories and the folks back home," Beal said in a late-night rap session. "Everyone back home thinks we're all over here doing hand-to-hand combat with Uncle Ho and the boys. They have no real idea or notion what's going on over here, let alone where to find Vietnam on a map or globe. As for the villages, well to most of them these places sound like little more than dropped silverware—Bong Song Bing or whatever—while to us the names have their own special meaning. The trouble is, they all think we're doing the same dirty job over here."

"So?"

At that the veteran grunt just stared at me with a quizzical expression and shook his head in disgust. Maybe he was wasting his time with me and the others.

"Boy, you are new, aren't you? Let me put it another way. It's like the Great San Francisco Earthquake of 1905—"

"Of '06," I said, correcting him. His quizzical expression changed to an annoyed glare.

"Whenever," he replied curtly. "The point is that the residents in the city at the time knew what was really going on, while the folks across the bay said they heard a terrible noise and were frightened for their own safety. For the REMFs it's the same thing. They hear the noise, see the smoke in the distance, and go home and tell everyone that war is hell and they don't want to talk about it; they share in our shit but don't want to step in it like we do. It has to do with front lines and proximity."

Sitting around the bare bulb that lighted the hootch, sipping cans of warm beer, we huddled around Beal, hoping to get a better understanding of the war and how it would affect us.

"I read somewhere there weren't any front lines over here," the PFC said, still having not learned his place in the scheme of things. For now, I was off the hook. I had only made a minor correction about something other than the war, while the PFC had stepped on it, the *it* being the male organ and the phrase applying to a GI's social faux pas. The PFC had a name now, not that it mattered since, other than by rank, last names gave way to nicknames anyway. His, he said, was Breeze. Not really a religious man, Breeze was covering his bet with the purchase of the Bible at the airport, like the ten-spot he'd put in the church collection plate on Sundays instead of going to confession on the Saturday evening before.

"What?"

"I said, I read where there ain't no front line over here, so what does it really matter where you are or what you're doing?"

Even though Beal knew the PFC's nickname, he wasn't about to recognize him in that way.

"New guy, new guy, new guy," Beal said rubbing his eyes. "In a week or so, when you're assigned to a line unit and you're out in the bush on patrol and when you hit the shit, I mean, when Charlie ambushes you and you're lying on your stomach in the dirt, hoping your rifle won't jam while thirty or forty of them are rushing at you yelling and screaming and firing their B-40 rockets and AK-47 assault rifles and thinking seriously about bayoneting your butt, I want you to think about the pizza stands back here, the go-go bars, steam baths, nightly movies, beer halls, and all the other fancy comfortable things like toilet seats and showers.

Then, I want you to think about the REMFs here enjoying them and that dumb-ass thing you just said about there being no front line."

"So how come you're going to be a grunt again, I mean, if you know better? Why aren't you a REMF?"

"Pride maybe, a sense of satisfaction of being in the infantry," Beal replied, "and the fact I couldn't lie, whine, or bribe my way into a comfortable REMF job. They may seem like dumb fucks to us, but they're smart enough to know just how good they got it."

Like most of the other young soldiers in the replacement station, I had no real idea why I was there or what, if anything, I'd accomplish. At nineteen years of age, I didn't really believe we were saving the world from Communism or Vietnam for the Vietnamese. I knew little of their language or culture, let alone the history of their thousand-year struggle against the Chinese, Khmers, French, Japanese, the French again, or the Americans and our allies.

Also, I didn't really think we were winning the war, either, since I'd overheard others with more age, education, rank, and experience say that it had already been going on longer than it should have. After all, Vietnam was a small country and not exactly a major power, so perhaps, as some had suggested, we were just testing new weapons, battle strategies, or even seasoning the troops using the "it's the only war we have, so let's make the most of it" policy.

So why was I there? Like some of my friends back home in Seattle, I suppose I could probably have maneuvered myself into college and out of the army, only I didn't want to because college didn't interest me as much as the war did. As any Saturday matinee moviegoer knew, war was exciting. It served as a rite of passage and test of manhood in too many popular films and books of fiction. The war in Vietnam already had been going on for nearly six years, and there were rumors that it would soon be over, so I wasn't so much afraid of going to the war as much as I was afraid of missing it! I had some friends back home who felt the war was wrong, while others said it was a matter of patriotism and of helping decent people who desperately needed help. All I knew was that I had to find out for myself. Action seemed better than inaction, so with all the bravado of any boy still in his teens, I enlisted in the army and volunteered for the infantry and Vietnam.

I had a certain fascination with war because I couldn't yet comprehend its consequences. I was too young and dumb to appreciate fear or the aftermath of hard-fought combat. It hadn't occurred to me that I might be filling the position of another, earlier, replacement who, just as cocky, just as foolish, had been killed by an equally young Vietnamese who was fighting for the liberation of his homeland, the freedom of his people and country, rather than worrying about his social status or any grand notion of vaulting into manhood. He would have a purpose while I would only have the war.

But then, I was still a new guy, an "FNG"—and not a "Funny New Guy," either, the way a writer in *Reader's Digest* had suggested—but rather a Fucking New Guy. The difference was that of cynicism as opposed to humor. Like other FNGs, I was still filled with illusions of petty glory and comic book heroics.

I signed for my rifle at the division's quartermaster supply shop. Like most rear-area supply storage depots, it was run like a general store, a tropical 7-Eleven for all the staples of war.

A sign on one of its two doors displayed its hours of operation. For those who worked there, the war was a nine to five workday.

A staff sergeant, watching our truck drive us and drop us off, eyed us with disdain. In a short, staccato speech he told us that we'd enter alphabetically through the door marked IN, pick up our gear, sign for our rifles, and exit through the door marked OUT. We were also told to keep the noise and grab-ass down inside, and once we got out he didn't give a damn what we did.

One by one we shuffled in and received our combat gear, which we loaded in a duffel bag and cloth laundry bag. Along with the rifle came all the necessary equipment needed by an infantryman to do his job, all that is, with one major exception—no ammunition. The quartermaster didn't want any overanxious young GIs bringing the war, or anything that remotely resembled it, closer to his safe and quiet shop. Too many of the new young hot dogs thought of themselves as tigers, and he preferred his tigers without teeth.

When it was my turn to sign for my rifle in the shop's large property book, I noticed the bold print letters KIA penciled in red across several signatures whose last names started with the letter J. The three letters, KIA, meant that the soldiers had been killed in action. An ominous note for an otherwise ordinary transaction.

"Take care of your rifles," the staff sergeant said as we exited the shop. "Otherwise, you'll pay for 'em!"

Thinking about the penciled letters KIA, yet another acronym we'd become familiar with, I knew that in one way or another, we certainly would pay for those rifles.

The staff sergeant was a black grunt from Chicago, a veteran on emergency leave and staying the night at the replacement station before he returned to his unit in the field. Several new arrivals were pushing to find out what the jungle was like and the war. He laughed at the questions; Beal only smiled. They knew the score, while the rest of us didn't, as yet, understand the game plan.

"You seen anyone get shot and killed?" a new arrival asked.

The sergeant smirked. "Shot and killed, huh? Well, man, if you only got shot at over here, then that wouldn't be so bad," the black sergeant replied.

"What do you mean?"

"I mean, there are a thousand and one other ways you can die over here as well. Besides getting shot, you can get rocketed, mortared, bombed, or bayoneted. Your helicopter can crash, your bunker can cave in, your jeep turn over, or a tank can accidentally grind you into ravioli. And before you ask, yes, the North Vietnamese Army has tanks down here. What else? You can get malaria, plague, dysentery, jungle rot, or die from a simple runaway infection."

Beal, sitting up in his bed, nodded to the vet. "Or you

can get rabies from a dog or rat bite, gored or stomped on by a pissed-off water buffalo or elephant, or bitten by any number of poisonous snakes, like the bamboo viper or king cobra."

The staff sergeant laughed. "Or you can die from heatstroke, heat exhaustion, or from being napalmed—accidentally. You can overdose on heroin or any combination of pills. You can step on a land mine, trip a trip wire to a booby trap, drink battery acid or ground glass that the Viet Cong have been known to put in GIs' beers. You can be cut, slashed, or flayed."

"What's more," Beal chimed in, "your pecker can fall off from any number of strains of VD, so whoever said a coward dies a thousand deaths while a brave man only dies once didn't take into consideration an active imagination."

"Or a keen grasp of the situation," the black veteran sergeant said, walking over to Beal and giving him the dap, the intricate handshake that originated with the black soldiers and had crossed over to many of the other veterans in the field. Meanwhile, the rest of us were laughing.

"Now, before you bust a gut, keep in mind that every one of these ways of dying we just mentioned, along with others we haven't even thought about, is ridiculously possible."

The black sergeant nodded somberly and then broke into a wide grin. "You see, war ain't only hell. It's a motherfucker."

# ACCEPTABLE LOSS
## by Kregg P. J. Jorgenson

Published by Ivy Books.
Available in your local bookstore.